Loose nEds

D0716432

Keith Waterhouse tells me that Yorkshire taxi drivers eclipse their cockney colleagues as conversationalists and I can believe him. He once had a silent pilot whose only words were: 'On the way I'll have to drop off a red cabbage on a friend of the wife's.' My man was much more chatty. He had an opinion on everything. On the ruins of Kirkstall Abbey, 'American women say, "was it bombed in the war?" I say, "Aye, t'war between Henry VIII and t'Pope".' On the sleek, shiny, futuristic black leather uniforms of the West Yorkshire police motorcyclists, 'Very kinky!' On the information that the new owners of Harry Ramsden's might franchise their product worldwide, 'Kentucky Fried Fish and Chips.'

About the author

Ned Sherrin is a regular broadcaster and host of the popular Radio 4 programme, *Loose Ends*. He is equally celebrated for his work in television (*That Was the Week That Was*), in films (*The Virgin Soldiers*) and in the theatre (*Side by Side by Sondheim*, which he devised and directed and in which he appeared in the West End and on Broadway). He also wrote many acclaimed novels and plays with the late Caryl Brahms, including *Liberty Ranch* and *The Mitford Girls*.

More recently he directed Judi Dench and Michael Williams in *Mr & Mrs Nobody*, Peter O'Toole and Tom Conti in *Jeffrey Bernard is Unwell* and Michael Hordern and Dinsdale Landen in *Bookends*, all dramatized by Keith Waterhouse.

From 1990 he wrote his own Saturday diary column for *The Times*, and in 1991 his *Theatrical Anecdotes* was a bestseller.

Loose nEds

Jottings from a fractured life

Ned Sherrin

Illustrations by John Minnion

CORONET BOOKS
Hodder and Stoughton

First published in Great Britain in 1990 by Robson Books Ltd.

Coronet edition 1991
Reissued 1992

Some of the material in this volume is based on articles which first appeared in *The Times* and *The Sunday Times* and are reproduced with the permission of Times Newspapers Limited. The story about restaurant bookings (p. 73) was jointly written with Neil Shand; the Bette Davis interview (p. 183) was first published in *Good Housekeeping*; the story about *A Fish Called Wanda* (p. 200) first appeared in the Scott's and Sheekey's anniversary magazine.

British Library C.I.P.

Sherrin, Ned
  Loose nEds: Jottings from a fractured life.
  I. Title
  828

  ISBN 0-340-55908-X

Printed and bound in Great Britain for Hodder and Stoughton Paperbacks, a division of Hodder and Stoughton Ltd., Mill Road, Dunton Green, Sevenoaks, Kent TN13 2YA (Editorial Office: 47 Bedford Square, London WC1B 3DP) by Clays Ltd., St Ives plc.

Loose nEds

Contents

For My Man in Deal

(who must remain anonymous in case we are ever asked to collaborate again).

Ned Sherrin Interviews Ned Sherrin

It is a daunting task to interview Ned Sherrin. People keep describing him as 'a wit', and yet in private he rarely says anything funny and, he confesses, the things he says in public are usually written for him by someone else. No matter how often he points this out people either assume that he is putting them on – or if they discover it for themselves they accuse him of concealing the fact.

Also, I have read some twenty 'in depth' interviews with Mr Sherrin, all of which were more or less identical – as was Mr Sherrin's autobiography, *A Small Thing Like An Earthquake* (Weidenfeld and Nicolson, 1983) – although the book is considerably longer. Moreover, Mr Sherrin has a reputation for being bitchy, sharp and impatient so, as this was only the second interview I had ever conducted with a (much misused word) 'celebrity', I set off for the World's End area of Chelsea in good time with some trepidation. I do not drive and could not afford a taxi, so I got to Sloane Square by tube and then waited for twenty minutes for the number 22 or 11 bus which Mr Sherrin said would bring me almost to his door. Finally, a number 11 appeared. In fact, six number 11s appeared, and I boarded the first. Like the other five it was almost empty. We sped along the still 'trendy' King's Road where purple-plumed punks rubbed shoulders with manicured Kensington matrons until I had travelled further down that road than I had ever been before – round the awkward bend and past the squat 'new shops' that line a housing estate until the bus dropped me, on Mr Sherrin's instructions, just short of the

World's End pub and near the Chelsea Garden Centre. I was
a little ahead of time so I took a turn around the Centre before
following Mr Sherrin's detailed map to his door. I had thought
to buy him a potted plant – of which he has said he was very
fond – to ingratiate myself, but I could find nothing sufficiently
impressive for so forbidding an interviewee, so I arrived empty-
handed.

Mr Sherrin lives on the first floor of a large mansion block,
built, I would estimate, at the end of the last century. Pleasant
gardens flank the macadam path which leads up to the front
door. The patch to my left was ablaze with a variety of cottage garden flowers – roses and hollyhocks predominated – a
pleasing splash of colour amongst the red brick which surrounded it. I pressed the bell to Mr Sherrin's apartment and
the answering buzz admitted me to a cool hall and a red-
carpeted staircase. Mr Sherrin greeted me himself clad,
rather surprisingly, in blue jeans and a pink denim shirt –
though for his public appearances he is usually seen in three-
piece suits. The informal garb has the effect of making
Mr Sherrin seem even fatter than he does on television,
where we do not see him as often as we once did (and when
we do it is usually in the afternoons). His welcome was brisk
and cheery and he offered me tea and buttered crumpets. I
do not normally eat crumpets but as Mr Sherrin had already
toasted a dish of these delicacies I decided that it would be
churlish to refuse.

Mr Sherrin lives alone. His flat is a sprawling affair. We
collected the tea tray from the small but fully equipped kitchen
and passed a minute guest bedroom. A plaque on the door
proclaims it 'The Grace Poole Suite' – apparently a humorous
literary reference which Mr Sherrin declined to elucidate for
me. The long central corridor hung with song covers of the
'hits' of the music-hall artist Marie Lloyd leads past the master
bedroom tastefully decorated in dark green with large attractive framed designs from one of Mr Sherrin's theatrical productions. The bed was unmade. Next we passed a bathroom,
functional but hung with posters from more of Mr Sherrin's

theatre shows, and then a utility room which was even more functional.

The passage opens out into a hall which doubles as a dining-room, with what looks like a Victorian pub table and six mock Jacobean chairs upholstered in a dull turquoise. Elaborate displays of glass walking-sticks in many shapes and colours which Mr Sherrin inherited from his late collaborator, Caryl Brahms, are the feature of the hall.

A small study and an even smaller library lead to the living room. Spacious, airy and light. Plainly, this is the result of 'knocking through'. Scattered around the imitation 'coal' fire are a comfortable sofa, a *chaise-longue* and a couple of arm-chairs, and a baby grand piano. The room looks out over the gardens and french windows give on to a small balcony. We admired the gardens below for which Mr Sherrin disclaimed any responsibility, giving the credit firmly to his neighbours.

Mr Sherrin poured tea and sat back to await my 'grilling'. Having read so many times that he is a farmer's son, educated at Sexey's School, Bruton, who did his National Service in the Signals and then went to Oxford and read Law, qualifying as a barrister and immediately joining ATV, in the 1950s, I avoided his early career. I followed the same course with his years at the BBC on the 'Tonight' programme, his invention of the notorious TW3 in the early 60s and his career as a film producer in the late 60s and early 70s (largely of off-colour comedies).

In 1977 Mr Sherrin went to America with the highly suc-cessful revue, *Side by Side by Sondheim*, and stayed for some two years appearing on stage and television. I suggested to Mr Sherrin that he had been rather old at 45 to embark on a career as an exhibitionist and he readily agreed but pointed out that as the British film industry was going through one of its 'bad patches' he had not had much choice. He said he had enjoyed America but preferred to live in England, though if anyone offered him a job in America he would probably be off like a shot.

By now Mr Sherrin had finished the crumpets and, though always polite, he was beginning to look at his watch. I asked him about his current projects. How, for example, did he get on with his youthful colleagues on the BBC Radio 4 award-winning programme 'Loose Ends'? Reflectively wiping a dribble of crumpet butter from his lower lip, Mr Sherrin gave a light laugh.

'Charming kids,' he said indulgently. 'In most cases I'm old enough to be their grandfather. Some people suggest that mixing with one's juniors keeps one young, but I find they add years to me.'

I asked why all the young men assumed working-class accents and all the young women spoke in upper-class tones. Mr Sherrin said that they were all hand-picked by Ian Gardhouse, his producer. He believed that Mr Gardhouse has a theory that properly-spoken young men are bad broadcasters, and that the same applied to improperly spoken young women. He was not sure if this is official BBC policy. I asked Mr Sherrin about his own rather studied (some say 'affected') tones, and he said he thought he must have had a Somerset accent at some time; but he couldn't remember when he lost it. Mr Gardhouse's prejudices about accents did not appear to apply to elderly broadcasters.

How does Mr Sherrin fit in all his activities? He said he did it by rising early and going to bed late and by getting Alistair Beaton or Neil Shand or his other collaborators to do most of the work.

It was time to go. Mr Sherrin had to change into a broadly striped blue suit to attend a first night. Although he had been unfailingly polite, I did not feel I had got to know much about the man behind the façade – probably no more than Mr Sherrin knows himself.

Side by Side by Sherrin

I do not intend to leave my present flat until I am carried out feet first in a box. I like it far too much. This melancholy glimpse into the near future was brought on by an exhibition of beautiful pictures of old Chelsea and the Thames at the Alpine Gallery in South Molton Street. One view could easily have been that from my window 125 years earlier, had my window been built then.

The Post Office and I are in dispute about my address, which they insist is Ashburnham Road, although a sign opposite my window clearly says Cremorne Road. Both these names echo the history of this bit of World's End. Would I have liked it more then than now? Cremorne Farm was at one end of Lots Road, and Ashburnham House roughly where the new yuppie-infested Chelsea Harbour complex now stands at the other.

We are a decorous set of citizens; but the land on which rows of Victorian terraced cottages now change hands at absurd prices once supported the last in the line of London pleasure gardens. Vauxhall gave way to Ranelagh, which was succeeded by Cremorne. Thomas Dawson, created Viscount Cremorne in 1785, converted his farm into the gardens. They were open to the public in the 1830s as 'the resort of a motley crowd of pleasure seekers'. Just down the road from 1990's Crazy Larrys (a disco for teenage bimbos) lay the haunt of earlier lager louts: 'Disgraceful scenes were carried on by those who were in the habit of meeting there.'

Another account of Cremorne is more complimentary. The farm was taken over by a rakish character called the Baron de

Beaufain, who had been inside after a Stock Exchange swindle in 1814 (they had those then, too). Sportsman, *bon viveur* and crackshot, the baron developed the land as 'The Stadium', a sporting club equally likely to stage 'Grand Miscellaneous Concerts, where the lovers of Terpsichore might sport the light fantastic toe'. George R. Sims remembered much later that the young bloods and the old bloods mixed freely. 'A noble earl would foot it featly with the festive mob ... and when the revelry degenerated into rioting, the aristocratic *viveur* would join forces with the common herd and would not think it beneath his dignity to exchange punches with a potman.'

These days we meet very few potmen down here; but I like the up-to-date style of one of the stars of Ranelagh, Lord Durham, a laid-back peer known as 'King Jog' because he once remarked that 'one can jog along on £40,000 a year'.

What I miss these days in Cremorne Road is the passion for ballooning which turned us into the Heathrow of the nineteenth century. Charles Green made 526 flights from here, including one in which he was accompanied by a lady with a tame leopard. One picture at the Alpine Gallery, by the famous Greaves brothers, who lived down the road on Cheyne Walk, shows the 'Cremorne' sailing skywards, watched by Whistler but not his mother.

Cremorne was shut down on 5 October 1877, and built over. Alf Brandon, a born-again tailor and Baptist minister, a 'Prude on the Prowl', published verses on 'the Horrors of Cremorne ... a nursery of every kind of vice'. Baum, the owner, sued him for libel. He won a farthing damages and no costs and was too ill to renew his application for his licence. At least Cremorne had not declined as had Vauxhall twenty years earlier when it was 'open to all ranks and classes, and a half-a-guinea will frank a fourth-rate milliner and her sweetheart through the whole evening'.

ON ARRIVAL IN Leeds to watch Timothy West splendidly recreating Sir Thomas Beecham for Yorkshire Television, I read

Willis Hall's column in the local paper. Recently in Italy his Florentine hosts showed Willis 'some canvases of Botticelli, Rubens and da Vinci' and introduced him to 'the delights of Tuscan cooking'. When they came to Yorkshire the Halls offered Ilkley Moor, the Cow and Calf Rocks, Betty's Café in the Grove in Ilkley and Harry Ramsden's famous fish and chip shop – with huge success.

Inspired to pilgrimage, the journey out to Guiseley was a satisfactory hors-d'oeuvre. Keith Waterhouse tells me that Yorkshire taxi drivers eclipse their cockney colleagues as conversationalists and I can believe him. He once had a silent pilot whose only words were: 'On the way I'll have to drop off a red cabbage on a friend of the wife's.' My man was much more chatty. He had an opinion on everything. On the ruins of Kirkstall Abbey, 'American women say, "was it bombed in the war?" I say, "Aye, t'war between Henry VIII and t'Pope".' On the sleek, shiny, futuristic black leather uniforms of the West Yorkshire police motorcyclists, 'Very kinky!' On the information that the new owners of Harry Ramsden's might franchise their product worldwide, 'Kentucky Fried Fish and Chips.' And on Yorkshire's idea of introducing non-natives into their cricket team – 'They had fifty new bowlers at nets t'other day. Thirty were Asian.' I suggested that they might find some slow bowlers in there. 'Need a few fast ones. 'Aven't 'ad one since Fred turned pundit.'

Harry Ramsden's was splendid. I had the 'special'. Fried haddock, chips and mushy peas. I have not had them before. On my return to London, Waterhouse boasted that he had been to Geale's Fish House in Notting Hill Gate on Monday to celebrate their fiftieth birthday – champagne and a jazz band thrown in. Well, I could have had champagne at Harry Ramsden's and at Saturday lunch there is a magician. But who wants to be flash?

IT IS NOT given to all of us to inspire a great novel; but such is my fate. It came about because I indulged in a childhood reminiscence on Radio 4. (Where else?) When we were very small my mother took my brother and me to Burnham-on-Sea. The principal excitement was a ride on a miniature railway. This ran near the beach on a small circular track and our enthusiasm knew no bounds.

A year later, when we returned to Burnham, we raced to the site of the railway. Desolate wasteland greeted us – dust, cinders and a few straggling fronds of willow herb. A lone stranger, observing our dismay, offered an explanation: 'A rich man bought it and took it away so that only his children could ride on it.' As I told Radio 4 listeners, it nearly turned me into a socialist on the spot – nearly, but not quite.

It was fifty years after our trip to Burnham that *No Train for Sam*, written and illustrated by Thelma Lambert (Gazelle Books, £2.99), landed on my desk with a letter from the author acknowledging her source. I read the blurb on the back: 'When Sam sees Ted's little red train touring the sea front he's filled with excitement – surely nothing can go wrong now to spoil things?' We, of course, know better.

I was disappointed to have my name changed to Sam, but artists must be allowed some licence and I had been given an Uncle Den, which is, after all, Ned spelt backwards. Ms Lambert concertinas her narrative a little; I (or Sam, if you prefer) leave the town for a few days in the middle of my visit. On my return, 'when Sam got to the sea front there was *nothing there!* No little train waited for passengers, puffing out blobs of smoke: no excited children clutching their tickets: no railway track ran along by the sea. The sign *Ted's Little Train* had been taken down and lay half buried in the sand ... Mr Crossman, who lived in that big house on the hill, had bought the train for his children.'

Of course, the story did not end there. Ms Lambert had some fine plot twists up her sleeve and I am not going to spoil them for you. You will have to buy the book.

IT WAS NOT my fault I was late for Laurence Olivier's memorial service at Westminster Abbey. I rose early, downed my fibre, dressed appropriately and did a little work. I ordered my car in good time. It was late. On the Embankment a van hit us up the backside. We inspected the damage. Just a bumper job.

By now the traffic by the House of Lords was jammed. I panted round the abbey to be told by a policeman that there was plenty of time. I went up a blind alley and finally arrived to find the great doors barred.

Led to an overflow seat in Poets' Corner between the memorials to Shakespeare and Garrick, I watched the tops of distinguished heads process to the sacrarium bearing the symbols of Olivier's life and work, and caught a reproachful shot of my empty seat on the television monitor.

His ashes were to be interred later in the artists' enclave which Chaucer inaugurated. In 1399 Chaucer took a lease on a house in the gardens of the abbey. When he died a year later he was buried inside its walls. Garrick lies there and so does Irving, courtesy of a last-minute reprieve.

On Irving's death the Dean of Westminster refused burial permission. But some years before, Sir Anderson Critchell, an oculist, had saved the dean's sight. He remembered the dean had offered any favour in return. He claimed Irving's place in the abbey and so Irving came to lie beside Garrick at the feet of the statue of Shakespeare.

Shaw, who received a ticket for the ceremony from Sir George Alexander, sent it back with a note: 'I return the ticket for the Irving funeral. Literature, alas, has no place at his death as it had no place in his life. Irving would turn in his coffin if I came, just as Shakespeare will turn in his coffin as Irving enters.'

One abbey epitaph catches the eye in a topical way. Written for Elizabeth I, Mrs Thatcher might care to remember it: 'Having restored religion to its original sincerity, established peace, restored money to its proper value ...'

CAST TO PLAY Miles, 'another servant', in Noël Coward's hitherto unperformed play, *Long Island Sound*, which was given a star-studded charity unveiling at the Theatre Royal, Windsor in the presence of HRH Princess Margaret, I found I had two speeches. The first was, 'Certainly, Mrs Murphy,' which I quickly mastered; the second was, 'Your Coca-Cola, Mrs Murphy,' on which I was working when we went into rehearsal. The problem was getting them in the right order.

The producer, Martin Tickner, rehearsed us in the stalls bar in the Prince of Wales and I heard a cleaner say, 'It sounds like a pantomime,' to which her colleague replied, 'Lionel Blair's in it. It must be a pantomime.'

Long Island Sound is *Hay Fever* on speed with a cast of thirty in the middle of a hectic American house party weekend. The longest roles were nobly borne by Robin Bailey, Caroline Blakiston and Lionel Blair.

Coward wrote it in his usual ten days and lost faith in it when close friends failed to laugh enough when he read it to them. At Windsor it offered gentle fun for an enthusiastic charity audience. My role passed off smoothly under the senior eye of Moray Watson, 'Higgins, a butler'. I was allowed a third line, 'Your martini, Mrs Grouper,' to Avril Angers, but I failed to get a laugh. Everyone else got theirs.

My next acting invitation was even more impressive. The Save the Children Fund was mounting *Joy to the World*, its annual Christmas spectacular, at the Albert Hall before the Queen and the Princess Royal. Major Michael Parker wrote: 'We are looking for volunteers to be Noah's grown-up children...' I asked if I could be Ham.

My acting career took a great leap forward with that, just when it looked as if I was in danger of being typecast. After giving my 'Awards Ceremony Presenter' for a Thames TV media serial and taping my 'A Radio Interviewer' for insertion in a new musical called *A Graveyard with Lights*, about the two brothers Wilson who went on hunger strike to save the Connaught Theatre, Worthing, I finally got to the Albert Hall to give my 'Ham, Son of Noah'. I think I had better quote my line. In one of Rosemary Anne Sissons's finest exchanges,

Noah (Stratford Johns) said, 'Here comes old Ham', to which I replied, 'Not so much of the old ham, do you mind?' Since you are unlikely to have seen it I can assure you I gave it full value; but Major Michael Parker's whole spectacular pageant was dominated by the surprise appearance of the Queen mounting the stage surrounded by children of all nations and delivering as a stand-up her very Green Christmas message to the world.

'NO, NO, TONIGHT you are a rich man's plaything,' the late, great Peter Bull once said to me. He was returning some trifling hospitality of mine by taking me to the movies and on to Prunier's for dinner. I had offered to pay for the taxi when we arrived at the Odeon, Leicester Square, and he was refusing to let me.

One weekend in November 1989 I really was a rich man's plaything. Sir Don Gosling, who long ago left the Navy to create his National Car Park empire, maintains his passion for the sea. The outward and visible sign is a yacht of some 520-odd tons moored at Antibes.

A gruelling assault course lay ahead. You wake at six to be taken by limo to Heathrow where you meet Elaine Paige and Tim Rice and board an executive jet. They were surprised and a little disappointed to see me as they confessed that had I not been there to play gooseberry they had ambitions to join the mile-high club. You breakfast lightly on lobster and smoked salmon canapés, croissants, orange juice and champagne. You are greeted at Nice at noon by Mrs Yusof, Sir Don's Girl Friday, and whisked to Antibes. Passing the similarly large yachts of Tiny Rowland, Peter de Savary and Alan Bond (for sale if you are interested) you board the splendid *Brave Goose* and meet the other guests: Rear-Admiral Michael Layard, his wife Elspeth, Robert Knight, Sir Don's solicitor, and his wife, Pamela, and Sir Don's mother, Maisie. My only regret was the absence of Sir Don's co-creator of NCP, Ron Hobson, but he was in Berlin, investigating the possibility of turning the Wall into a multi-storey car park.

You down a Bloody Mary or so in the upper deck saloon, stroll on to the sun deck and admire the old port before settling down to a lavish luncheon – avocado and crispy bacon, roast beef, for it is Sunday, and baked Alaska. Then you are allowed to sleep for a couple of hours, the water gently lapping at your porthole, before gathering in the saloon for cocktails (a mean vodka martini in my case).

As it is the last weekend of Sir Don's season, you go into Cannes with the entire crew for an evening of fine food and frenetic celebration at La Chunga, which has been taken over for the night. Coincidentally, the band plays two hits from a new French musical which Tim Rice has just translated, so he is inspired to join them in a selection of Elvis's greatest tracks and several encores of 'Ob-la-di Ob-la-da'. Then you find yourself steadying a tiny table, on top of which the beautiful lady purser from the yacht dances without inhibition. You return to your luxurious cabin and know no more until 10am when you look through your porthole and observe the shore slipping away as the yacht glides towards the islands off Cannes.

Transferring to *Little Goose*, Sir Don's baby boat, you meet a Dulux dog running wild on Honoré, inspect the Abbaye de Lerins and buy a pot of lavender honey from a nice old monk. *Little Goose* also has champagne on ice so the visit is not too privational. Back on *Brave Goose* you must eat a splendid brunch with sinful fried bread, before being whisked back to Nice, your executive jet and London.

Quite frankly I could view a career as a rich man's plaything with equanimity.

Domestically, that was not a peaceful period. Two house guests crammed my flat to bursting point. One, David Yakir, an American executive from an advertising firm, Ayer, phoned the entire world. The other, Kevin Sharkey, who was between apartments and is a songwriter among other things, had had his new single released by Boney M. I have never wanted to dance like Josephine Baker but this record declared that everyone does and so insistent was the tune that after you had heard it about 200 times you began to believe it.

Driven out of the house, I found myself conducting informal research into our education system with particular reference to the teaching of history. The standard was disturbing. The King's Road had been full of children pleading 'penny for the guy'. Before handing over I had taken to asking them who Guy Fawkes was. Out of ten enquiries I had one correct answer: 'He wanted to blow up Parliament.' The most outré reply was: 'He was Captain Blood.'

Two little girls outside the chemist's thought hard and one came up with: 'He was Mrs Thatcher.' The other corrected her. 'No, no, he was an old man Mrs Thatcher wanted to murder,' she said, with a blood-thirsty smile.

ALTHOUGH I HAD not intended to buy one, it has never been my practice to look a gift dish in the mouth particularly when White Sands Holidays informed me I had won a cruise or a week in the Bahamas for two or a trip to Disneyland for my partner and me and our two children or a dish and receiving apparatus.

All I had to do was phone the company and be somewhere between teenage and decrepitude. I just qualify inside the upper limit.

I made an appointment for 2.30pm on Saturday at 10 Great Marlborough Street, despite dire warnings from my Radio 4's 'Loose Ends' team that I was going to be bamboozled into buying an expensive time-share.

However, White Sands said there were no conditions and I took it at its word. A crowd of us sat around on low sofas. An elderly couple clutching Selfridges bags looked ex-colonial. Indian parents and a small child watched apprehensively, and a seriously overweight doctor needed help to rise when his name was called.

Several dapper young men buzzed in and out with

clipboards. Mine was called Mark. He led me briskly to a white table for a briefing.

I had promised to give up an hour and a half of my afternoon. First we had trouble defining my job. Butchers, bakers and candlestick makers were all there on his form, but there was no jack-of-all-trades section.

He moved on to holidays – where did I take mine? I told him I didn't.

'Never?'

'Not if I can help it,' I said.

Then why had I come? To get my dish.

Mark looked flummoxed. He summoned his superior who quickly admitted defeat. I was taken to another Mark and processed.

I was soon out in Great Marlborough Street again clutching my voucher. I would have to pay for the installation, but I would be saving £300–£400 and all the goodies that Sky Television can offer would shortly be mine.

There must be a catch in it. There was, but not of White Sands's making. I phoned the agents for my block of flats to see if there was any problem about erecting a dish.

Yes, they said, the lessors and all my fellow tenants must agree. Even if the tenants said yes, the probability was that the lessors would not.

The prospect of nightly communion with Derek Jameson and Frank Bough receded and I resigned myself to being dishless in Chelsea.

NOT ALL THE mail I get from appearing on radio or television is abusive. H G Rasmussen wrote to compare me with a Danish actor, Christian Gottschalk. I wish I could have found the courage and wit to come up with Gottschalk's gesture in a performance in Copenhagen at the beginning of the war.

According to Mr Rasmussen, 'Christian Gottschalk came on stage with his right arm straight up in the air and faced the audience. Several young German officers jumped up and lifted their arms in a "Heil Hitler" salute.

'Gottschalk stood still for another few seconds, then he said, "The snow was *that* high outside my front door this morning," leaving a laughing audience and bewildered German officers.'

IT WAS HARD to go anywhere at Christmas without bumping into Dame Vera Lynn. It was also a great pleasure, but I had thought to namedrop a sentence about the Duchess of York. However, no sooner was I raising a glass with her slim, tanned grace than Dame Vera was at our side. Our rendezvous was the Hyde Park Hotel, where the Berkeley Square Ball organizers were handing out the splendid sums they had raised for charity.

A few days later and there was Dame Vera again at the Grosvenor House for the television and radio Christmas lunch addressed by Frank Carson, who tells 'em almost as well as Mike Yarwood.

My network of insider information collapsed that week as My Man in Deal had gone down with flu, like so many elderly persons. In his case a symptom had been a morbid urge to dwell on the history of his complaint.

I thought the flu was a nineteenth-century affliction but no, Hippocrates knew all about it in the fifth century BC. Until 1743, it was known here as *la grippe* (it still is to Adelaide in *Guys and Dolls* – 'A person can develop *la grippe*', she sings of her cold).

However, in 1743 John Huxham encountered it in Naples where Italians called it *un influenza di freddo* or 'an influence of the cold'. Huxham latched on to the word 'influenza' and brought it home to England where it flourished. Epidemics were blamed on travellers from Russia until the pandemic in 1918 when it was compared with the Black Death. Twenty million people died, more than perished in the First World War. The next big scare was the Asian flu epidemic of 1957 which was traced to China, via Hong Kong refugees.

Asian flu was a popular complaint through the 1960s and once it did me a good turn. When we were producing the movie *The Virgin Soldiers* in Singapore, my colleagues Leslie Gilliat and John Dexter and I were disturbed to hear that an executive of Columbia Pictures was planning to pay us a visit on location. I knew him as an enthusiastic collector of jade and reckoned he wanted the company to fly him east for free. The only way he could justify the expedition was to solve a crisis, so he set about creating one. He spotted the word 'lesbian' in the script and announced it would be unacceptable on home screens in America. He must fly to sort the problem out.

This is just the sort of trouble you don't need when you are making a film. We pondered how to deter him. Fortunately I also knew he was a king-size hypochondriac. I wired our delight at the prospect of seeing him, advised him that we had reserved the plush Golden Dragon Suite in the best hotel for him and added that he must get all possible Asian flu shots as an epidemic was raging.

My telegram arrived in the middle of a Columbia board meeting in downtown Burbank. It passed the length of the table. The other vice-presidents read it as they moved it down. 'Well,' said the last VP as he handed it to our man, 'I guess you won't be going.' We were left in peace.

THE WEDNESDAY BEFORE Christmas was not a good day. There had been John Birt's Christmas drinks at the BBC on Monday with Janet Street-Porter and Archbishop Runcie coupled handsomely in conversation. Then 'Loose Ends' partied on Tuesday and I went on to carols at Claridge's: but on Wednesday I was due to speak at a concert in memory of Joan McMichael Atkins who died in 1989, 24 years after founding Medical and Scientific Aid for Vietnam, Laos and Cambodia. I was also making an artichoke and parsley soup. I like to have a good thick soup on the go at this time of the year. Just as I was finishing the soup David Smart, who organizes

MSAVLC, phoned to say he was looking forward to seeing me the next night. 'No,' I said, 'tonight.' 'No,' he corrected me, 'tomorrow.' I gave in, put down the phone and poured the thick artichoke and parsley soup all over myself.

However, Thursday worked out all right. I sandwiched St Paul's in between David Hatch's BBC radio party and more ravishing carols at Ronnie Driver's dinner at Haberdashers' Hall.

At the concert Julie Christie was doing translations of Vietnamese poems; and Luigi Palumbo, classical guitarist, Judith Fittons, flute, and the Roussel Trio, the Dulwich College string quartet and the WMA singers completed the line-up. I exhumed an old 'BBC 3' script. Peter Lewis and Peter Dobereiner wrote *The Song of Lyndon* in the same year that Joan founded her charity. It was the only time Hugh Carleton Greene censored one of our scripts on the three 1960s satire shows. Relations between Downing Street and Portland Place were strained and Vietnam was a particularly sensitive area. I phoned, memoed and even wired the DG but he refused to budge, and verses which savagely attacked Lyndon Johnson's policy and Harold Wilson's complicity in the manner of *Hiawatha* were not performed. So Thursday marked its début.

'... Friends we have but one objective:
Human life must be safeguarded
So today I have directed
We at once resume the bombing
And because our aims are peaceful
We will bomb them twice as often.'
From across the deep blue water
Words from little Harold Wilson
Warmly backed up this decision.

If my attachment to the *Song of Lyndon* took me back to 1965, the nostalgic trip I took the next day transported me to 1952. That year Norman Riley was the business manager of *Dick Whittington*, Oxford University's Dramatic Society Pantomime. The other day he was turning out a drawer and came across the old programme. He had the inspired idea of a reunion lunch. He was in time to round up Leonard Webb, now a playwright, the original book writer and director; Philip Dale, now a translator and occasional pianist at the Garden House hotel in Cambridge, then our composer; Raymond Cooke, now a Cliff Adams singer; and the original Dick, Nigel Lawson, now a politician, then a slim chorus boy, and me, now me, formerly fairy queen.

We met in the Crown Passage Vaults and shared whitebait and sausages and mash. Nigel was sparing on the mash and envied Leonard Webb, who arrived wearing the corduroy coat he had worn through rehearsals. Neither Nigel nor I would get halfway into the clothes we wore then. We pressed the late chancellor about his memoirs but he would only say he was about to buy a word processor. I reminded him that Jimmy Carter wiped eight chapters of his autobiography, but Nigel said he was going to take lessons. We appointed ourselves as a steering committee for a proper 40 years' reunion in 1992 with absent friends rounded up. The brokers' men were Wallace Olins, now *the* specialist in designer management (he was abroad) and Bob Gavron, now a publishing magnate (he was lunching at All Souls). The cat (Jeanne Lewis) was in Sweden. I knew where two more members of the chorus, Liz Robertson and Dick Chapman, were, and surely Deirdre Reid, who did the décor, is now Lady Rosebery. We badly needed to find the lyricist, Don Collis, who was a chemist. One of his songs, 'More spoils from the oils', sounded prophetic to Nigel, and lots of the lyrics were rattled off verbatim.

> Any Arab with a scarab
> His weapon has to yield.
> He regards any woman as an arable field
> And they all judge her worth by the size of her
> Down in the tents of Arabia!

We were obviously determined to be up to date in 1952.

There were even knowing references to cocaine; but I prefer this simple joke. I can't recall its context; 'What about the Swiss Alps?'

'A wonderful place for a yoyo.'

PEACE BROKE OUT quite often between the various children at Hickstead Place, where I spent Christmas with Douglas and Mrs Bunn and all the others. The main problem was that Chloë (nine), Daisy (seven), Rose and Sonny (five) all wanted to play with presents given to Charlie (three). Only Ned II (15) and Arabella (less than one) held aloof.

Charlie's remote-control car and his portable space invader were the principal bones of contention; but in the end they all found alternative ways of amusing themselves.

Chloë was translating 'Twelve Days of Christmas' into Greek. Daisy cleaned out a toy stable and Rose was given to mournful dramatic soliloquies delivered through the banisters from half-way up the stairs. Charlie himself ran a lot, Arabella smiled and gurgled, and Ned II mused with dignity on a broken arm suffered from falling off an elephant.

The grown-ups also had tasks to perform between eating and drinking. Peter (medicine) joined me in my traditional position as official maker of Bloody Marys and may have usurped it; Ross (journalism) was i/c emptying ashtrays and made a fine fist of that after it was pointed out that he only had to throw away the ash and not the tray as well; Larry (property) dogged our host's footsteps to the wine cellar in the grounds and was responsible for carrying and later pouring. Douglas decanted himself.

For those interested in what we drank with Christmas lunch there was a St Emilion, a Trotte Vieille 1964 with a chic black and gold label; a Margaux '66 (with a modest cream label with the château picked out in gold); a Gevrey Chambertin '61 (label missing); and an Anjou, a Moulin Touchais '59 (label white, identification spelt out in black).

You will notice that I have not described the wines. This is

for two reasons. They were all wonderful and I am no good
with words such as buttery, earthy, tannin, fruity or nose. Also
we had a total of seven large meals over four days and so
Christmas lunch was but the tip of the iceberg.

Other featured wines included a Romanées Conti '82, a
Rieussac '80, a Hennessy Grande Champagne '62, Cockburn
'50 and Croft's '63. Jane MacQuitty should ask to inspect Mr
Bunn's cellar as soon as she can. There was also a magical old
Madeira, bottled in 1920 but Douglas thought much older,
and either because of it or in spite of it some dreadful things
were done late at night to a Jason Donovan poster. I suspect
Mrs Bunn.

My final duty at Hickstead was to hand round drinks at a
Boxing Day party. The first year I did it, one guest congratulated Mrs Bunn on her wisdom in hiring a servant – 'So
wise to get a man in to do it.'

But my three best squelches that year did not happen in
West Sussex. Keith Waterhouse wrote a play, *Jeffrey Bernard
is Unwell*, I directed it, and Peter O'Toole played the part of
Soho's living legend – drinker, gambler and *Spectator* columnist. Not long after its opening at the Apollo Theatre, I was
at a Groucho Club party for Jeffrey Bernard's *Low Life* paperback, Auberon Waugh asked me: 'Have you *seen* this play of
Bernard's?'

At a music publisher's luncheon, a woman said: 'I wasn't
expecting to enjoy your speech but I was agreeably surprised.'

And, best of all, a very pleasant publicist, who had been
escorting Peter O'Toole to an interview with Melvyn Bragg,
reported: 'I'm a bit worried. Peter kept referring to "Ned" and
I am not sure if anyone will know who that is.'

As the year proceeded my identity crisis got worse. At
Manchester airport a professional driver advanced towards
me saying hopefully, 'Professor Murgatroyd?' In Portland
Place a despatch rider asked after my two sons and when
I suggested nephews – of which I do have two – he said,
'You are Desmond Wilcox, aren't you?' Inside the BBC I
presented myself for a broadcast in studio 3D. The re-

ceptionist rang through and told them, 'Benny Green is here.'

LOOKING FOR ADVANCE information before visiting Australia for the first time, I made the mistake of consulting My Man in Deal, who was last there with the Navy in 1945 when large oysters were half a crown a dozen, when there wasn't a high-rise in the place and the pubs shut at six. The time between 5pm, when city offices closed, and 6pm was known as 'the bastards' rush'. He reported that the scene at five past six was not a pretty one. The beer was fine, the wine quite good, but 'the gin burnt the woodwork – crook guts, sport!'

It is not like that now, so why is he telling me?

I did, however, like his story of a party to which he was invited in Melbourne. The hostess complained that some joker had written 'Philip of Greece' in the guest book. Her touchiness was explained by the fact that a mobster in Sydney, much in the news at that particular time, was known as 'Phil the Greek'. What she did not know was that Prince Philip and his cousin, Lord Milford Haven (who were both lieutenants in the Navy), had crashed her party. As it happened, Phil the Greek was shot soon afterwards. His nick-namesake more wisely returned to the United Kingdom, married, and lived happily ever after.

Anyway, I acclimatized on the plane by spreading the Veg-emite thick and plundering the Australian news sheets. I pre-pared myself for unnatural heat, punch-ups between police and Aborigines and a strange new vocabulary. In the *Sydney Morning Herald*, Jodi Whiting (16) pronounced on the New Year celebrations: 'Last year it was really "grouse". This year it was just boring.' If grouse means good it will describe my journey.

As we Qantassed our way comfortably across the sub-con-tinent, waking fitfully, I swear that from 33,000 feet I caught a glimpse of the Taj Mahal in floodlight if not moonlight and, yes, it did look like a biscuit tin, Amanda.

I was in an English colony. Victor Spinetti was already here. Elton John was expected. Mike Batt is artist in residence at the Sydney Conservatoire. Ivor Spencer is teaching young Australians how to be butlers and there is an invasion of European wasps (*Vespula germanica*). These had been there since 1958 and were believed to have arrived via New Zealand in a crate of Second World War aircraft parts.

I was welcomed with three iced lime daiquiris at the Sydney Festival Club in the grounds of the Hyde Park Barracks, a beautiful building which started its ugly life as a convict prison. Music was pounded out by a rock group called Fargone Beauties (say it aloud in a heavy Australian accent).

Thirty hours after waking in World's End I fell asleep in the spare room of my host, Ken Groves, in Potts Point, Woolloomooloo.

I'd gone there to open Victor Spinetti's one-man show at the Playhouse Theatre in the Sydney Opera House complex and to host a two-continent edition of 'Loose Ends' 24 hours after I landed. A 10am transmission in London means a 9pm start in the Antipodes.

At 8pm I was in the middle of a cocktail party at the Copplesons, whose handsome house in smart Rose Bay has a spectacular view up the harbour towards the glowing sky-scrapers of north Sydney. The foreground picture beyond the garden wall is white sand and big, friendly, strutting grey gulls.

Those who know me were not surprised to hear that I nearly failed to make it to the 2BL ABC studio in King's Cross. ABC shares this neck of the wood with the famous red-light workers. I was assured that Rose Bay was a mere five minutes away and that it is the easiest place in Australia to get a taxi.

As I waited, the heavens opened and giant stabs of electric storm carved up the sky. I huddled under an awning, joined by a pretty girl who described herself as a model. We agreed to share a cab. I dropped her in pouring rain at the corner of Williams Street. It was now that the driver decided he did not know where 2BL was and suggested I hunt for it on foot.

Yes, he did understand I did not know my way, indeed he had felt much the same recently in Norway when he found himself stranded with a backpack and a broken leg. As he drove off I saw two friendly ladies of the night standing by the kerb in bright plastic macs. They had never heard of 2BL. When I returned after circling the building a few times, they had been replaced on their beat by two even more friendly statuesque six-footers with much deeper voices and no better information.

By now it was 8.45pm and, considerably bedraggled, I spotted the box-officer of the tiny Crossroads Theatre, advertising Frank McGuinness's play *Observe the Sons of Ulster Marching to the Somme*. I reckoned that any company with the nous to put on a play which won a *Standard* Most Promising Newcomer Award would know how to get to a radio station. They did.

A fascinating interviewee on the show was Valerie Taylor, a shark photographer who worked on *Jaws I* and *II*. She has had her leg bitten through by an Ocean Blue which she was tempting with minced mackerel far off the coast of California (he preferred leg to mince), her hand gnashed by another and her chin opened up by a frenzied Grey Nurse Shark off Queensland. She firmly believes in shark conservation.

For all the sophistication of Sydney and its imaginative building developments, circling sharks, blazing bush fires, crook crocs, blinding lightning, burning sun and bronzed bodies are a constant reminder of the nearness of nature.

I THINK I celebrated my 59th birthday on the right day. I hope it was the right day. My birth certificate says 18 February but a family Bible has the 19th. As I was the second son, no one can remember at precisely what time of which day or night I happened along. It makes it tough for astrologers.

However, the cast and crew of 'Loose Ends' gave me a birthday card for the 18th and stuck on two horoscopes. Both are high on Mercury. One says he would 'inject (me) with brilliant brainwaves, inspiring instant insights, imaginings and ideas'. According to the other, Mercury gives me 'the gift of the gab as well as imparting verbal expression to (my) ingenious mind and incredible notions … cerebrally (I'm) in a class of (my) own and way ahead of (my) time.'

I was lucky to celebrate my birthday by launching a charity. The British Sports Trust had allied with Scott's of Mount Street and the champagne house of Krug in arranging three-monthly banquets celebrating the best seasonal fish washed down with three sorts of bubbly. A £100-ticket gave a chance of three draws. Winners got a dinner for seven guests; losers' money to the Sports Trust.

My onerous task was to summon some guinea-pigs for a test run. I chose my cast carefully. Elisabeth Welch is a champagne connoisseur and had a vintage named after her in the 50s. Keith Waterhouse qualifies, if not as an expert, certainly as a conspicuous consumer – along with Jean Leyland, his flame-haired factotum. Victoria Mather and Reggie Tsiboe got in on looks and conversation. I had a slight problem with the Tom Contis, as Mr Conti has a seafood allergy and Mrs Conti doesn't drink alcohol.

THERE WAS ONLY one day in a busy month I could get down to Somerset to rescue a few things from my brother Alfred's farmhouse before he retired on Lady Day 1990. We had been there since 1934. David Sedgman, the new man, was already ploughing up fields I walked in or worked on as a child. I had a last look at evocative acres with names like Larkswhistle, Stockwell, Ploughmeads, Copythorn and Langlands.

A catalogue advertised 'Highly Attractive and Genuine Dispersal Sale of Three Tractors, Toyota Land Cruiser, Farm Machinery, implements and effects'. They were lined up in the Home Field. Harrows, cultivators, scythes and sickles rubbed blades with a sheep foot-bath, two of Lampert of Somerton's finest tipping trailers and old cider barrels.

There was a group called 'Bygones', now good museum fodder but mostly implements with which I can claim first-hand acquaintance from my childhood. There was the 'twin-screw Cider Press c/w frame', a 'Day of Mark' Apple Mill, a winnowing machine, the 'Long Single Twin-Furrow Horse-Drawn Match Plough, with press wheel' with which Herbie Bown used to win ploughing matches, guiding Jolly the chestnut cart-horse, or Captain, Bonny or Prince (various shades of black and grey). They would return festooned with rosettes attached to the shining brasses on their polished harness.

The bean droppers, the bull tether and the hay sweep stood alongside the hay elevator, which the farm men christened 'Ned' because I could not lift the bales and invariably had recourse to it.

My brother unearthed a copper-plate inventory of the last Sherrin sale on my grandfather's death in 1903. Same auctioneers. Some of the bygone items appear in it, bought in then by an uncle. The bean dropper fetched six shillings, the apple mill five, and the winnowing machine three guineas. I hoped Alfred would do better.

In fact the winnowing machine went for a mere two quid.

HENRY JAMES PROBABLY got it right. 'Almost everyone interesting, appealing, melancholy, memorable, odd, seems at one time or another after many years and much life, to gravitate to Venice.' It took me much life, little appeal, no melancholy, some oddness and 59 years. I should by rights have gone six years earlier, when I wrote an article, 'Noël and Cole in Venice', for the Orient Express magazine. I neglected to claim the fee I had negotiated – two round trips. At David Frost's garden party I bumped into James Sherwood, who revived the famous train. Just as I began to press my claim another guest said what bad form it was to discuss business at a social event and steered him away. Fate intervened when I talked after dinner to executives of Sealink (a sister firm) in Eastbourne. I elaborated on my sense of grievance. Some time later we embarked.

I asked an old friend, David Yakir, who is an advertising whiz-person with the Ayer agency in New York, to come along. Yakir, a Brooklyn Jew, invented the faintly tiresome concept that we were two old Jewish widowers, Solly and Eddie, making the journey in the evening of our lives. This fiction was temporarily punctured at Victoria when I was asked for my autograph. The man produced two cards, one to sign, and one which proclaimed him 'a private enquirer with 24 years CID experience'. 'Keep that,' he said. 'You might find it useful.' My personal Poirot!

The Solly and Eddie personas reassembled ('we usually go to the Catskills – they throw in Jackie Mason'), we were treated royally *en route* to Folkestone, but at our age we found getting on and off the cross-Channel boat a slow anti-climax. Like Queen Victoria, I yearned for the Channel tunnel. Way back in 1858 Thomé de Gramond showed Prince Albert a design which prompted the Queen to write: 'Tell the French engineer that if he can accomplish it I will give my blessing in my own name and in the name of all the ladies of England.' Palmerston put the kibosh on that. England, he said, was far too close to the Continent already. Frustrated, I remembered Chips Channon, who wrote in his diary on 20 February, 1936: 'Sir Arthur Colefax died today. He was a good man; talented, high idealed, but boring beyond belief. Lord Berners once said of him that he "had been offered £30,000 p.a. to bore the Channel tunnel".'

Although living quarters are cramped on the Orient Express for two arthritic old gents – Solly, the younger, had the top bunk – the care of the crew and the luxury to hand are as proclaimed. We were given twenty-four hours of brochure-like perfection by one David, from Louisiana, who had at least a dozen of us to look after and a boiler to stoke. France looked just like France when we went to sleep and we awoke to find Switzerland looking exactly like Switzerland. Paris, Zurich, and St Anton yielded a more cosmopolitan batch of travellers, and I wondered for a long time about the tragedy behind the remark I overheard as the lobster arrived: 'I really regret taking Denia to the Grand Canyon.'

Each compartment has a dinky little wash-basin but naturally no shower so by the time we got to Innsbruck the scent of cologne, deodorants and body rubs lay heavy on the Tyrolean air.

You are supposed to judge the sophistication of Orient Express travellers by who is reading Agatha Christie's epic and who has plumped for Graham Greene's *Stamboul Train*. I counted one of each. Failing to get a freebie all the way to Stamboul, Greene bought a ticket to Cologne. He says that keen readers will notice that there are fewer details of the journey in the latter part of the book. Just before it was published J B Priestley threatened to bring a libel action because he identified himself with Mr Savoy, the popular novelist portrayed. Greene had to share the cost of preparing the new pages in thirteen thousand copies. 'No law suits, please, Solly,' I pleaded.

Back in 1929 Evelyn Waugh wrote in his travel book, *Labels*: 'What can I possibly write, now, at this stage of the world's culture, about two days in Venice, that would not be an impertinence to every educated reader of this book?' Include me in. But I have to report that poor old Solly, misled in his dotage about European converters, had blown his American video camera and moaned about it as we passed every schloss and chalet, and boarded each gondola and vaporetto. At least it spared me hours of embarrassing posing. Then he failed to make his still camera work. However, I did find the perfect restaurant. Keith Waterhouse had lent me an enchanting guide book – J G Link's *Venice for Pleasure* (1984 edition). On page 151 Mr Link recommends the Vecchia Cavana, 'favourite restaurant of that celebrated gourmet, Mr Bernard Levin'. It was charming. Seeking to ingratiate myself I pointed out the glowing tribute. 'Ah! Signor Levin!' said the delighted waiter, and hurried away to fetch the *maître d'hôtel*. They returned in triumph bearing a Polaroid picture. 'Signor Bernard Levin!' they chorused triumphantly. Unfortunately the snap was of Signor Sammy Cahn, the distinguished lyricist of 'Three Coins in the Fountain'. We had not the heart to disillusion them, faced as we were by a massive antipasto of prawns, *latticini*, freshly-baked crab, tender mussels and clams, followed by Risotto alla Marinara, spaghetti sauced with more seafood,

tomato and herbs, a green salad, and a mixed platter which
included sole, *bosega*, monkfish, lobster and sea bass. *Saz-
zoppino*, a sort of house sorbet of cream, vodka and lemon
juice preceded the *tiramisiu*.

We did what we could in the time. We circled the Bridge of
Sighs, we marvelled at churches, pictures and a cornucopia of
Canaletto views. We inhaled the evening mist in St Mark's
and were deafened by the clatter on Sunday morning. We had
the ritual bellinis at Harry's Bar and coffee at Florian's. We
inspected the traditional fussy, filigree glass and admired the
simple, elegant, modern, Murano designs. Early on Sunday
morning we made a pilgrimage to San Michele, where Diaghilev is buried. According to John Kent's colour guide to Venice,
Gore Vidal spotted that the two pink ballet shoes (by Capesio,
'Dancing Since 1887') on the little memorial are both for left
feet. This huge island cemetery (Napoleon's idea) is dotted
with sad cypresses under which thousands of Venetians are
laid. Immediately inside the gate the hand-painted wooden
sign points to the grave of three famous foreigners: 'Ezra
Loomis Pound, Strawinsky and Diaghilew' (sic). Passing
countless children's tombs decked with flowers and touchingly
illustrated with photographs, we found the latter two in a quiet
Russian enclave. A bunch of fresh celandine sat on Diaghilev's
plinth, some tulips on the plots of Stravinsky and Vera. The
weather had ravaged the pale pink pumps. I examined them
closely. How Gore could tell they were both left feet is a
mystery. Wouldn't it have been easier to obtain a pair? Who
was the young dancer who put them there and when? Are they
replaced as they decay? In the *New Yorker* at the time of his
death, Janet Flanner, Paris correspondent, wrote: 'Diaghilev
had only 2,000 lire to his name at the beginning of his last
illness and hoped by dying quickly to die within his means:
but bills to Venetian chemists and hotel-keepers left him a
posthumous pauper. It is said he was buried through the
generosity of his friend Gabrielle Chanel, the famous and loyal
dressmaker.'

About the shoes, no one suggested to me who put them

there but Nadia Nerina rang to tell me that Gore Vidal, as author of *Death in the 5th Position*, should know better. Ballet shoes are made to be worn on either foot and quickly adapt to the dancers' shapes. She thinks the shoes on San Michele must be replaced regularly when they disintegrate – just as someone regularly places flowers on Pavlova's grave in north London. When Nadia took Ulanova to visit it some years ago, the blooms were fresh and neatly arranged.

I doubt the devoted buncher is the dancer who featured in one of Caryl Brahms's favourite stories. An English member of Pavlova's company, she was standing in the wings one night when the music for *The Dying Swan* began. Before the great ballerina could make her solo entrance, the girl made hers. Afterwards she explained that she had an irresistible urge to express herself in the dance, and was greatly surprised when Madame sacked her as soon as she came off.

ONE OF THE great joys of Easter weekending at Hickstead, apart from Christopher Biggins' technicolour waistcoats and a fashion-conscious young father pondering 'What shall I wear to push Arabella's pram?', was the healing presence of Sky Television.

Deprived of my own dish I was starved of live Test cricket from the West Indies. Here was a chance to assess how much of Vivian Richards' irascible behaviour could be traced to his painful complaint.

There is ample precedent for calling it by its proper name. When he was Foreign Secretary, Ernest Bevin went into hospital for what the Foreign Office spokesman delicately described as 'an internal operation'. Bevin was not pleased with this euphemism. He said bluntly: 'Call it piles, lad.'

Noël Coward was similarly frank and fascinated. He was operated on two days before rehearsals began for *This Year of Grace*. He was furious when the papers called it 'a minor operation' and declared: 'If that was a minor operation, I should have been far happier with a Caesarean.'

However, he got on with writing the second act of *Bitter Sweet* and his favourite visitor was Dame Marie Tempest. While others, 'seldom referred, except obliquely, to the mortifying nature of my complaint'; she 'came on several occasions to see me and we discussed every detail with enthusiasm.'

Evelyn Waugh so admired the grandiloquent English on the old Bromo boxes proclaiming a cure for 'that distressing and almost universal complaint THE PILES' that he tried in vain to the end of his life to acquire one of them. His trip to America to promote *Brideshead Revisited* was delayed by his encounter with the knife. Later he told his biographer that after all the chronic pain, 'The operation was not necessary but might conceivably have become so later on.' Christopher Sykes was astonished. 'Not necessary? Then why did you have it done?' Waugh gave the splendid reply, 'Perfectionism.'

In trying to project myself into Viv Richards's frame of mind I recalled my own experience in the 60s. As the first post-operational moment of release approached my nurses at the London Clinic assured me it would take place at 9.30am exactly. Loyally I waited. At 9.25 they wheeled in a mahogany throne on to which I was hoisted. Suddenly all hell broke loose. Nurses I had never seen before crowded in from all over the clinic to enjoy my suffering. Then my secretary banged on the door to announce that she had brought my letters and refused to go away. At the moment of most extreme pain 'Housewives' Choice' on the radio struck up with the old hymn 'All Things Bright and Beautiful'.

Yes, at that moment I could have hit a journalist.

TOO LATE IN life I discovered the rigours of charitable badge selling. The Red Cross launched an assault on Oxford Street and although I was hardly in the van, I collected my box, sash and official accreditation immediately after 'Loose Ends'. I chose smart, boutique-ridden South Molton Street as my first beat, but I hadn't bargained for the quickened steps, the averted eyes, or the three Chinese yuppies who fled screaming into a taxi at the sight of a collecting box. In New Bond Street a taxi driver gave me a generous quid, but pointed out that I had no Red Cross sticker to give him. I slunk back to base and collected four sheets of stickers. It was a hot, balmy day, and the secret is to catch 'em sitting. Café tables dominated James Street and St Christopher's Passage, and I was grateful to the lunchers who dipped deep into their pockets to get rid of me quickly.

I AM NOW, I think, unofficial, unpaid literary consultant to *Sunday Sport*. For those who do not also subscribe to that tabloid, it is a fantasy publication which specializes in discovering Elvis Presley alive and aliens from outer space in unlikely places.

'DICTIONARY bosses were in a spin last night,' the anonymous author wrote on 4 June, 'after super *Sunday Sport* brought them a new word ... GOBSMACKED. Book boffins are so shocked that we've made the word POPULAR, they want it put in the *Oxford Dictionary*.' It means amazed, astonished. First they called Sarah Tulloch, 'a senior editor on the *OED*'. She said: '*Sunday Sport* has done a lot to make the word popular. Gobsmacked will be put forward for inclusion.' The paper goes on to boast its other contributions to our literary heritage. 'First we brought you STUNNAS with big WHOPPAS. Then HUNKS sporting massive MANHOODS ... now GOBSMACKED is likely to join the 500,000 words contained in Britain's 20-volume dictionary.'

This, via a telephone interview, is where I came in. 'Satirist and TV personality Ned Sherrin reckons Britain's favourite family newspaper has saved the word from EXTINCTION.' Mind you, they didn't use all my expertise on the word, or at least half the word. Gob as spittle goes back to the sixteenth century. We had the gift of the gob, not the gab, in the seventeenth century, and in the eighteenth century the Scots picturesquely called a mouth a gob-box, and the English turned the silver spoon into a gob-stick.

In the nineteenth century gob went down the social scale into racier company. A gob-spud was a potato held in the mouth to round out sunken cheeks whilst shaving (I must try that), and a gobful of claret was a boxer's bleeding mouth. As a child I enjoyed gob-stopper sweets. The *Sport*'s attribution of the phrase to a northerner ambitious to be a comedian, Bernard Manning, is rash.

A Bit of a Do

Although I once ate at the same table as Sir Geoffrey Howe at a dinner, I was quite a way from him and next to Lady Howe, which some people say is even more fun. Unfortunately, just as we were beginning to let our hair down, our host, John Birt, the deputy DG of the BBC, made one of those power-host moves and pushed all us men four places round the table. This deprived me of Elspeth Howe but gave me a splendid view of a brand new coupling in the far distance, where Peregrine Worsthorne had landed up next to the enchanting Tessa Sanderson – better known for her prowess with the javelin than for her attendance at the High Tables of Oxford or the Chancellories of Europe.

I once had dinner with Sir Robin Day and the late Hermione Baddeley, an occasion confused by Day's determination that Baddeley was a music-hall singer and his attempts to get her to join him in several choruses of 'Any Old Iron' and *her* insistence on talking politics to him – a subject on which her knowledge was nil.

I began to fantasize a similar misunderstanding between Worsthorne and Sanderson. 'Really loved your editorial, Perry, absolutely fantastic!'

'Thank you, Tessa, my dear, how about joining me for some field sports ...'

Dinner with the Princess Royal at around the same time was also a slight exaggeration, though we both had smoked salmon and watercress roulade, lamb and pineapple as guests of Bafta in the banqueting hall in Whitehall – the place with unhappy memories for King Charles I. The ovation for the Princess Royal after what must have been a couple of difficult days was so long that her first sentence was: 'Can I sit down now?' But having been refused permission she gave, as usual, a brisk, informed and to-the-point plea for corporate support for film and television arts. I was sitting opposite Lord Grade who, at 82, appeared to have the year 2000 most on his mind. He was planning a special celebration which Arnold Hammer, a mere child in his 90s, has promised to attend. Lew wants his own epitaph to be 'I didn't want to go'.

That was also Sir John Gielgud's reaction to the happy lunch at Whitbread's Brewery near the Barbican which was given in his honour for the benefit of the valuable Mander and Mitchenson theatrical collection. I can't quite understand why the Press made such a fuss about Gielgud's absence. Surely at that age you can make up your own mind? Two years earlier they honoured Lord Olivier, a mere stripling then of 80, and he didn't come either.

Punters still had a splendid time, with a rich array of Knights and Dames, and although they were denied first-hand Giel-goodies (Emlyn Williams's inspired invention to classify Sir John's dropped bricks) they were treated to two new ones at secondhand from John Mortimer. One was personal. Years ago Mortimer and spouse arrived at a grand dinner party with a very young baby in a carry-cot. Gielgud was a fellow guest. As the Mortimers left he spotted the baby in the cot. 'Why did you bring it with you?' he inquired loftily. 'Are you afraid of burglars?'

The second story was professional. Sir John is not at home on a horse. During one film a fledging director asked him to advance his steed two paces and then to speak his line. For ten takes Gielgud said the words perfectly but the horse did not move. The young and patient director pleaded: 'No, John, I want the horse to move forward two paces *before* you say the line.' 'Ah, yes,' Gielgud said, 'but does the horse know?'

I was handed a letter at the lunch. It was from Timothy West, who could not be at the lunch, to Donald Sinden, who could. Tim was recently in a taxi. The driver said words to the effect: 'You're an actor, aren't you? I've had 'em all in my cab.' (So far it sounds like Henry Root, taxi driver.) He went on to attack the acting talent of Larry Hagman. 'I've 'ad that JR from "Dynesty" (*sic*). Terrible actor!' Tim West politely demurred. The driver was not impressed. 'Not like his mother, Maisie Martin.'

'No, Mary Martin.'

Driver: 'Yes, it just goes to show, it's not always handed on.'

Tim: 'What do you mean?'

Driver: 'Well, look at Thora Hird and Donald Sinden.'

Sinden was very sporting about not having inherited Thora Hird's talent.

MANY YEARS AGO, I got home one night to find a message from Vanessa Redgrave asking me to join a march for unmarried mothers the next day at Hyde Park Corner. I am not sure if we were to walk in favour of more of them, or for better treatment of those already with us; but feeling that I probably

had less direct responsibility for unmarried mothers than most of my contemporaries, and having in any case to return to filming on the location of the inaptly named *The Virgin Soldiers* the next morning, I failed to answer the call. It has left me with mothers, married and unmarried, on my conscience.

The years between have sometimes spurred this conscience into frenzied activity. Birthright is one of the charities for which I occasionally turn out, and one week I was asked by George Pinker, the president of the Royal College of Obstetricians and Gynaecologists, and his wife to dine at the college in Regent's Park to discuss a concert I was to introduce in July starring Thomas Allen, Rosemary Ashe and Siobhan MacCarthy. It was to open an international medical conference in the presence of the Princess of Wales for whom, I understand, Mr Pinker did the business. Since the conference was worldwide, the music had to be British.

I remembered how I had failed Vanessa. I remembered my recent complete inability to recall my first kiss (in response to a National Aids Trust request for information on that subject for a fund-raising book for Christmas); and I set off.

I had done some research in order to cross knowledgeable forceps with the doctors. (Forceps were invented by a Huguenot refugee family called Chamberlen in 1569. Two sons were obstetricians to the courts of James I and Charles I. Needless to say the physicians objected.)

I had prepared other conversational gambits. For example, sixteenth-century midwives were often burned for witchcraft on account of their 'gross female sexuality'. Joseph Priestley discovered laughing gas in 1772, and a Scottish obstetrician first used chloroform on the expectant Queen Victoria in 1847. I reckoned that would get me through the asparagus.

Now, I know Mr Pinker has only entered the lists with recent generations of royal babies; but I wanted to find out if the Home Secretary still hangs around during royal deliveries. It must have been disconcerting for the Queen Mother to have had old Joynson Hicks at 17 Bruton Street, when Sir Henry Simon was delivering the Queen by Caesarean. Princess Margaret provoked even more inconvenience. She was due to be born at Glamis Castle in late August, 1930. The Home Secretary, J R Clynes, arrived on August 5. Lord Strathmore couldn't bear the idea of having a socialist politician under his roof, possibly for weeks, and palmed him off on a kindly neighbour, the Dowager Lady Airlie – where he still was when little Margaret Rose arrived 16 days later.

My curiosity was of no avail. Mr Pinker is an old Gilbert and Sullivan buff. When he was a medical student at St Mary's he was Pish-Tush in *The Mikado* – the man who brings news of the Mikado's decree that 'young men might best be steadied' if 'all who flirted, leered or winked/unless connubilally linked/ should forthwith be beheaded'. (A poor look-out for unmarried fathers.) Not content with playing a leading part, young Pinker rang the Palace and invited the Queen and her two daughters to the show. They accepted immediately. Panic reigned at St Mary's. The performance was nowhere near up to scratch. An SOS was sent by the D'Oyly Carte and relays of experienced Savoyards turned out to coach the medicos. The performance was a great success, and the nearest I got to asking an informed question was if it was his singing that got Pinker his job as Royal Surgeon Gynaecologist? Modestly, he said it was not.

UNTIL I WAS asked to present the prizes at the Collins Dictionary/Times Crossword Championship I had no idea that the modern crossword was devised for the *New York World*'s Sunday supplement, 'Fun' as late as 21 December 1913. The inventor was the editor Arthur Wynne, an English immigrant journalist. The puzzle was diamond-shaped. There were no black squares and the first clue was, 'What bargain hunters enjoy' (5). I can't solve it. Perhaps our winner, Dr John Sykes, a lexicographer with OUP, can oblige. It was 1930 before *The Times* succumbed to the craze. How did actors while away their time at rehearsals before then?

One finalist got married the day before the contest and the sponsors kindly subsidized his wedding night at the hotel. Not surprisingly, he slipped in the ratings from eleventh last year to seventeenth.

Again jokes were offered. It was the anniversary of the start of the Second World War, so I gave the joke prize to the former diplomat and musical buff who came seventh. 'Hitler's dilemma in 1939,' he said, 'was what to do first, finish off Poland or polish off Finland.' Almost a re-run of a joke that went the rounds in New York when the Polish singers Jan Kiepura and Marta Eggerth opened there in the 1940s in *The Merry Widow*. After the performance an anxious Kiepura asked a fan if he should polish up his English. 'No,' said the fan, 'English up your Polish.'

I WENT TO a spectacular fund-raising party for Sam Wanamaker's Globe Theatre which started at the Phoenix Theatre where those established Shakespearians, Michael Caine, Bob Hoskins and Robert Powell, enjoyed Dustin Hoffman's Shylock and so did everyone else. I fell to wondering in what roles Sam Wanamaker, mastermind of the Globe, might cast them. Hoskins has already played Iago on television for Jonathan Miller, but since Iago was an officer not an NCO, we can't have him doing that again. He'd be good opposite a dog, so it's Launce in *Two Gents*. Powell, an obvious Romeo, is perhaps a bit long in the tooth now, so he will make do with Benedick. The choice for Caine is the most obvious. Polonius has a line to Hamlet: 'Do you know me, my lord?' 'Excellent well, you are a fishmonger.' Now, not many people knew that – so it's Hamlet for Caine. Afterwards at the Savoy, to which we were red-bussed, we had Venetian antipasta, Venetian chicken and gondolas of exotic fruits. Wanamaker made a lively plea for funds and I could not help but draw parallels between this glittering black-tie occasion and the previous night's cosy nostalgic party at Sadler's Wells to celebrate Colin Chapman's book about Unity Theatre – the far-left amateur group which flourished from the 1930s to the 50s. Bob Hoskins started his career at Unity. He liked drinking at the bar and one night he was dragged on stage. The stock drama which Unity regularly revived was Clifford Odets's *Waiting for Lefty*. I first saw Sam Wanamaker in the early 1950s in Odet's *Winter Journey*. Both boys have come on since then.

One of the highlights of the Unity cabaret was Lionel Bart's 1955 song about a Soviet race horse called 'For a Lasting Peace'. Maybe *glasnost* will inspire a disc revival now that Lionel is a hit again.

YOU FIND ALL sorts at a party for Peter Ustinov, which is not surprising since Mr Ustinov is a bit of a mixture himself.

Having long known about his Russian, German, French and
Italian blood he now tells me that there's some Ethiopian in
there as well. It was a jolly party at Morton's in Berkeley
Square. Terence Stamp, Ustinov's protégé in *Billy Budd*, was
there as an author in his own right, but he still greeted Peter
as 'master'. Marguerite Porter, the dancer, also has a new
career as an author and the man from Channel Four's breakfast time programme tried hard to get me to say that actors
should not write books. No luck. Anyone who thinks Ustinov
can be limited to one career has small purchase on reality.

One disaffected actor who has *not* written a book was
spreading a naughty rumour that Trevor Nunn's new musical
The Baker's Wife should be rechristened *The Director's Wife*.
Mrs Nunn plays the title role.

This is the latest of those satirical reworkings of show titles
like *The Glums*, *The World of Woozie Song*, and Alan Lerner's
last Broadway show, *Dance a Little Closer*, which finished up
as *Close a Little Faster*.

I had not heard a joke name for *Miss Saigon*; but Cameron
Mackintosh says that when a researcher rang the Vietnamese
Embassy to check on local wedding rituals she was asked for
what purpose. She explained that it was for *Miss Saigon*. 'No
such place,' said their man at the embassy, 'that is Ho Chi
Minh City.' Somehow I don't think that Miss Ho Chi Minh
City is going to sing.

It being a literary party there was not much discussion of
books; but David Jessel picked on Humphrey Carpenter's *The
Brideshead Generation* which perpetuates the myth that Harold
Acton invented Oxford bags. In the windows of Hall's in the
High Street there is a card which quotes Lord Boothby: 'Credit
for inventing Oxford Bags is generally given to Harold Acton.
This is not so, I, with Hall Bros in the High Street invented
them myself. Since this was the only creative achievement I
did at Oxford I felt I should be remembered and I must claim
it.' I called Mr Carter, who was 79 and joined Halls in 1928.
He agreed with Boothby. In 1989 they started making bags
again. They sold at £160 a pair.

Alan Crompton Batt, guru to the restaurant trade, enthused about how easy it was to publicize Loyd Grossman's new restaurant. On entering you were as likely as not to see Loyd Grossman reading an article by Loyd Grossman about how good Loyd Grossman's new restaurant is. It cut out the middle man. New restaurants proliferated. The Caprice boys were to reopen the Ivy, and Howard Malin, a director of Morton's, had both a new film and a new restaurant about to burst on us. The restaurant, off Hanover Square, was called Caspers, and featured those table-to-table telephones so popular in *Cabaret*. At a trial run of the restaurant, Malin spotted three young men at one table, dialled the number, and, affecting a girl's voice, said: 'Would you like to come home? My husband's away.' He got a unanimous response: 'We'd rather come round when you're away and your husband's at home.'

THE EXCITEMENTS OF *Miss Saigon* began as I settled into my seat behind Mary and Jeffrey Archer. 'How considerate of the management to put short people in front of us,' I said. 'How considerate to put fat people behind us,' snapped Mary, who is perhaps going for the 1989 Dorothy Parker award. ('Age before beauty,' said Claire Boothe Luce once, standing aside to let Mrs Parker past. 'Pearls before swine,' replied Mrs Parker as she swept through. I also like George Kaufman's gesture at the first night of a particularly awful play. He asked the women in front if she would please put her hat back on.)

The party at the Cotton Centre was an oriental delight. It cost about five times the entire budget of *Jeffrey Bernard is Unwell*. Riverboats shuttled guests across the Thames. The champagne flowed; but not quite fast enough for Peter Cook, who came back bearing a bottle he had filched from a waitress on an ingenious pretext: 'Excuse me, Melvyn Bragg is causing a bit of a disturbance over there, I think this will pacify him.' In fact, Bragg was being as good as gold, oddly lamenting to Mel Smith and me that younger novelists of the Martin Amis generation take themselves far too seriously.

IT WAS A fine day for the races. There were long queues at the Tote windows. The sun lit the white Tattersall Stand across the course, and a few horses galloped by to the start. The bookies rubbed out and altered the odds as the horses went by, their hooves padding like boxing gloves on the turf...

If you think my prose is improving you are not wrong. That paragraph is Graham Greene. Pinky went to the races in *Brighton Rock* and so did the actors in *Jeffrey Bernard is Unwell*, chaperoned by Mr Bernard and Mr O'Toole, who both breathe racing.

Jeffrey has foresworn making a book since they got him for evading betting tax in the Coach and Horses. However, we had a conscientious cast, and using the thorough rehearsal methods of Mike Leigh, they wanted to research betting with Jeff as bookie, and experience everything up to but not including his arrest.

While O'Toole went off to place grown-up bets, we gave our pounds and fivers to Honest Jeff.

Bernard has his own way of tempting trainee punters to back a doubtful animal, a string of beckoning phrases: 'Although Moonwarrior hasn't been placed for two years, I hear he is improving rapidly ... I don't know why you are choosing Pussyfoot ... Cotton on Quick will sew it up ... I can't understand why intelligent people around this table are ignoring Pink Pumpkin... There's only one horse in this race, you can forget the rest ... they shouldn't bother to open the [adjective] stalls for the other [nouns]... This race was designed by the Jockey Club to give Otterburn a nice afternoon...' and my favourite: 'Ridgiduct is trained at Melton Mowbray. What I want to know is, why has he sent it such a long way?'

As it says in the play, 'people shouldn't listen to people, should they?'

Eventually we rumbled that Jeff hadn't even bothered to lay off our bets until Keith Waterhouse did Alysardi in the fifth race. Seeing our commission agent now hastening towards the big bookies we all backed it, too. We all won.

Jeff summed it up: 'Inside the last furlong, that horse was

doing handsprings. As they say in Yorkshire, it was catching pigeons!'

In the last race Waterhouse collected £80 on Harken Premier ridden by Brian Rouse, the first jockey we had seen on our arrival. Betting on such a person is an old racing superstition. It certainly spoilt Jeff's game plan. Our turf accountant's final word was a vivid verdict on racecourse waitresses (those at Brighton excepted): 'A torrent of talcum powder cascades over your roast lamb.'

As we were leaving, a strange woman in a trilby hat shouted at me: 'Are you still living with Mary Knox-Johnston near Biggin Hill?' I am not and never have been, which will come as a relief to Ms Knox-Johnston.

AUTUMN IS THE season of mists and mellow launchfulness. A rare puritan impulse kept me from a publication party for *The Glory of Champagne*, but I did catch up with a curious new phenomenon. Have you been to any good bottle launchings yet? They are the coming thing.

Back in the 60s, when *A Funny Thing Happened on the Way to the Forum* opened here, the authors Burt Shevelove and Larry Gelbart were asked to a series of dinner parties. Breast-feeding was newly fashionable and at the first their hostess, Julie Andrews, who was at that time married to the designer Tony Walton, skipped pudding and brought out her new baby for a snack. The next night the then wife of Richard Pilbrow, a producer of the show, did the same. The morning after Larry called Burt and said: 'Are we booked into any good breastfeedings tonight?'

Bottle launches are not as glamorous. The first bottle was designed to hold a French mineral water, Volvic, which was unveiled at Christian Deltiel's restaurant, L'Arlequin. M Deltiel is from the Auvergne and so is the water. A witty girl from *The Caterer and Hotelkeeper* magazine, Lorna Pettipher, wondered about the etiquette of bottle launching. 'Should we crack a ship across it?' she said.

Bottle two was delightful too. It was unveiled along with the new Egon Ronay/Cellnet *Guide to Hotels and Restaurants* at the Savoy. All sparkling spring water tastes the same to me – this one came from Tynant, Lampeter in Wales, and the design is worked out on a computer by a man in Yorkshire. Its shape is not unlike a Perrier bottle, but it is the most beautiful blue – almost as beautiful as the blue of Bristol.

Robin Shepherd, who commissioned the design, thinks it is even more attractive. I doubt if Lazarus Jacobs or his son Isaac, who had a famous glasshouse in Temple Street, Bristol in the 1750s, would agree. Before the old boy died in 1796 he was advertising himself as 'glassmaker to King George III'. Today he would be glassmaker to Nieman Marcus. As well as toilet bottles, scent bottles and patch-boxes, he produced a strangely shaped, dark blue 'boot-glass' named after Lord Bute, the much-disliked local landlord and politician who was Prime Minister for one disastrous year – 1762–3. The relevant toast was 'Down the boot'. The secret of the 'blue' in Lazarus Jacobs' glass was achieved by the use of smalt (a kind of cobalt) imported from Saxony. Mr Shepherd was not disclosing his special ingredient.

THE ONE THING that great movie *Lawrence of Arabia* lacked was a title song. Indeed, when it first hit the screen we plugged the gap on 'TW3'. David Kernan sang a rousing 'Yippie-i-o!' number by Steven Vinaver and Carl Davis about T E: 'Riding through the desert/On a camel's back.'

It went on:

> Dressed up like an Arab
> Camping in a tent
> Dreaming of his Molly
> Waiting back in Kent
> Wild and free-ee!
> Good old T E-ee!
> Lawrence!

Surprisingly, it never caught on; but I was reminded of it when I presented a Critics' Circle award to the composer Maurice Jarre for lifetime achievement in the cinema and for *Lawrence* in particular. Unfortunately M Jarre (who, incidentally, composed the first *son et lumière* score for Chambord and look where his son, little Jean-Michel, has taken that genre) was busy in Hollywood, so the prize was picked up on his behalf by George Fenton.

M Jarre once gave George a piece of advice on scoring movies. He told him to take a wife or girlfriend to recording sessions because they are always full of disagreeable producers making trouble. The presence of a woman, he counselled, makes these horrors behave better. Fenton said ruefully that he had tried it but, when he did, it had always been the wife or girlfriend who then behaved badly. He added that he suspected the much married M Jarre's experience had, in reality, been similar.

It was an affable low-key affair. Susan Fleetwood gave Daniel Day-Lewis, garbed like a Dickensian undertaker, the award for best actor. Sir Alec Guinness took a special gong from Ronald Harwood for 'the brilliance of his long career'. Sir Alec has just come back from a Venetian holiday and, when I said I went to Venice for the first time on the Orient Express, he looked severe and cautioned me against the cost of laundry at the Gritti Palace.

Ronald Harwood had two splendid stories of obsessive artists. In Morocco, Dustin Hoffman had him sit through a video of his *Death of a Salesman* performance before dinner, fast forwarding the bits between his own appearances; and once, in Malibu, Rod Steiger screened his original television role as *Marty* upside-down because he had failed three times to lace up the film properly. 'You can watch it this way,' he barked in the end and, craning their necks at an awful angle, they did.

Finally, Christopher Hampton, who took the best screenplay award from Colin Welland, confessed that all that rubbish in the Sunday papers about his identifying with an isolated character in an alien environment for his television series *The Ginger Tree* was eyewash; his main incentive for taking the commission was the lure of three weeks in Japan to which he had never been.

Greater love for his readers hath no elderly person than to turn up at the Hippodrome at midnight on a Thursday. I gave it 15 minutes. I examined the tacky Star Bar – a misnomer if ever I heard one – and left my sequin-jacketed companion to dance the night away.

I read later in a London evening paper that I had been in the presence of Curiosity Killed the Cat, 'Fast Eddie', whom I do not know and Eddie Kidd, whom I know and like; Alan Pellay ('glossy and black and wreathed in chains') – I know him; Tyree (never heard of him/her) and Steve Strange as compère.

Our reporter wrote that the men wore 'smart casual clothes – pressed jeans and sports jackets'. Surely smart pressed jeans are a contradiction in fashion terms? My style guru Robert Elms confirmed that this is the ultimate in anti-chic.

I left with a backward glance, hoping perhaps to glimpse the ghosts of Bobby Howes, Binnie Hale or Billy Milton, or the spirits of Ivor Novello and Margaret Rutherford in *Perchance to Dream*, even Cicely Courtneidge in *Her Excellency*; or perhaps Judy Garland and Ethel Merman who played there when it was the Talk of the Town, but the noise and the DJ had frightened them off.

A demo that week was more fun. The King's Road Traders were up in arms about the rent increases (up to 300 per cent) which were threatening the character of the street. One Saturday morning they rallied at a buffet lunch at Raffles, in company with a curious cross-section of interested parties. Alvin Stardust, a regular customer at Stephen King's clothes shop for men, rubbed shoulders with Nicholas Scott, the local Tory MP, while Stan Newens, our Labour MEP member, was in earnest discussion with Richard (*Rocky Horror*) O'Brien.

The irony is that 30 years ago the King's Road was a perfectly ordinary, quiet, small town street. The escalation of property values has nothing to do with the enterprise of the landlords and everything to do with the energy and imagination of the traders.

I dare say some residents would prefer a return to the small town thoroughfare, but what they are likely to get is a creeping invasion of large multiples who are already advancing from Sloane Square like some science fiction blob.

ON ONE OF those winter gale days, John Dankworth and Cleo Laine hosted their annual Wavendon All Music Awards – presented by their most loyal supporter, Princess Margaret.

More than once she had to reassure herself that the scaffolding on the building next to the Banqueting Hall, in Whitehall, was not going to attack us as we lunched a few feet away from the scene of Charles I's execution. What with that, and her plane being struck by lightning at Gatwick, the weather was not being too kind to HRH.

Ronnie Scott, an award winner, told a terrible tale of the last big blow. Not known for his true stories, he swears a friend lost his panicked dog on that awful evening. Early next morning the hound returned with the neighbour's dead pet rabbit proudly held between his teeth. Scott's friend guiltily washed and blow-dried the rabbit, scrambled over the garden wall and replaced it in its pen.

Later he was visited by the neighbour, visibly distressed. He asked if all was well. 'No,' said the neighbour, 'just as our son was getting over the death of his pet rabbit, which we buried yesterday, some swine's dug it up, washed it and put it back in the pen.'

Cleo sang a cabaret after lunch, including two Arthur Young settings of Shakespeare lyrics. Princess Margaret and Steve Race learnedly debated if this might be the first time they had been heard in that setting since the days of Inigo Jones.

In dereliction of duty I forgot to check with John a story which Neil Shand told me. The Dankworths once performed at Carnegie Hall in a classy promotion for a new Japanese car.

Also on the bill were an infant prodigy and Itzhak Perlman, who caused some confusion among the sponsors when he announced that his first piece was by Kreisler.

The next day it was the turn of the ballet. Nadia Nerina celebrated Sir Kenneth Macmillan's sixtieth birthday for him at the Berkeley Hotel. As well as Lady Macmillan she had corralled Dame Ninette de Valois, Irina Baronova, Alexander Grant, John Lanchbery, Nicholas Georgiadis and Yolande Sonnabend for a menu divided into three acts. Lanchbery has a Beecham story which I had not heard before. He was present when Sir Thomas overheard Sir Henry Wood complaining, and muttered, 'Oh dear, more whines from the Wood.'

Dame Ninette was in fine form. We had a spirited disagreement about the future of Drury Lane, which she thinks should stop being a home for musical comedy whenever the ballet needs it.

Touching on the competition between ballet and opera inside the Royal Opera House, she recalled an old visiting Russian dancer asking: 'Between opera and ballet here in England, is also Montagues and Capulets?' When she assured him that it was indeed, he went away much heartened at finding this phenomenon universal. She also remembered a wartime tour of *Swan Lake* in Scotland when a woman berated her for cutting *The Dying Swan* – never in the ballet anyway.

Madame Baronova's reminiscences were more personal – like her elopement with her first husband. Jerry Sevastianov was one of Colonel de Basil's managers and Baronova, still a baby ballerina, was restless under her parents' strict discipline.

As the company moved from Cleveland to Cincinnati, de Basil arranged for her to speed ahead with her beau straight from her performance. By the time parents and company caught up with them in Cincinnati, the marriage was a *fait accompli*. Baronova insists she was so naïve on her wedding night she kept her husband waiting while she put her hair in curlers.

HORTICULTURE LED ME (yes, I know what Dorothy Parker said and I can't think) to tent city at the Royal Hospital. Hitherto I had only seen the Chelsea Flower Show on the fag-end of Friday, but this time I sneaked in while stands were still getting their finishing touches. Brogued and tweeded ladies, ex-colonel lookalikes and horny-handed lads in jeans and muddy trainers were conspiring to give the temporary plots an air of permanence before the Queen arrived.

The favourite publicity trick for exhibitors is to name a flower after a celebrity. Sure enough, there at the entrance was Gertrude Shilling being photographed beside her eponymous yellow rose, her face peeping out of a mass of silk petals lovingly arranged by her hatter son, David. Unfairly, the lace across her face prevented her champagne glass from reaching her lips. 'Didn't they name one after you?' I asked Penelope Keith, as she wandered by. She dismissed the idea airily, 'Oh, that was five years ago.'

Elsewhere, champion namers were at work. Over the years, S & N Brackley of Aylesbury has called its sweet peas after Noel Edmonds, Terry Wogan, Esther Rantzen, Alan Titchmarsh and Percy Thrower. This year its pea-person was Su Pollard, who cavorted amiably for the cameramen, professing as much excitement about her unique honour as Mrs Shilling about hers.

Over at a fruit and veg stall, looking for signs of mad broccoli disease, was the politician of the week, John Gummer. People may be calling him names but no one named as much as a beetroot after him. I suggested it was unchristian to be paying so much attention to non-biblically approved vegetables, when Mr Gummer launched into a vicious attack on the Brussels sprout. (It gives off all sorts of noxious chemicals when cooked.)

He should have checked with the Carnivorous Plant Society, whose leaflets encouraged growers to meet and compare carnivores. I had a vision of little Gummer lured into a Venus fly-trap by a beefburger.

The Belgians had the biggest but most boring exhibit;

Guernsey the most ambitious – an old mill by a stream; North East Fife Recreation Department the most bizarre – three calves and a stag at bay made out of bronze chrysanthemums. My palm goes loyally to Kelways of Langport, Somerset, for its irises in a spectrum of rusty shades.

By noon, the red carpet leading to the president's tent was unrolled and the sun was tickling the bricks of the Royal Hospital. 'Quiet and dignified,' Carlyle called it, 'the work of a gentleman.'

WHEN AMBASSADOR CATTO and his wife instituted a series of screenings at the American Embassy even one Sabbath became social in my humdrum round. I blotted my copy-book right away by mistaking Peter Plouviez, the General Secretary of Equity, for Alan Sapper, who does the same for the ACTT. Then I sowed some doubt in Mrs Catto's breast by wondering which of Richard Gere's new films – the nice one or the nasty one – she was screening. She said she was sure it was the nice one because the ambassador only liked happy endings. She was right. It was *Pretty Woman*. The start was even happier: after the salmon and chicken we were americanized with large bags of popcorn and I shall retain the image of Lord Stevens of Ludgate, Shaun Plunket and their ladies solemnly munching their corn in the stalls alongside Elaine Page and her leading man, John Barrowman. Mr Barrowman is an all-American Scot and was suitably concerned about one imperfect tooth in an otherwise dazzling set of molars.

KING CONSTANTINE'S BIRTHDAY do in and around Spencer House was very jolly. Lady Elizabeth Anson is an old hand at running these things, but planning a massive pink marquee with a placement for 650 guests on a raised ballroom floor, with field kitchens underneath, sounds a nightmare to me.

The royals were apportioned at one per table. The Queen had the one nearest the dance floor. At our table we drew the

Earl of St Andrews. This was a particular distinction, as I learnt later he is the one member of the family whom David Frost has not met. King Constantine pretended irritation because his son's speech, dwelling on the king's youthful indiscretions, went better than his own.

Before dinner I bumped into a delightful Greek who was admiring the flamboyant restoration of the Great Hall of Spencer House. 'It is a wonderful job – and I know, I am in construction,' he said. I ventured a comment on the cost of this sort of thing, reminding him of the trouble there was in doing up the 'marble halls' of the Ritz. They had to bring craftsmen out of retirement to achieve it. 'Ah,' he nodded sagely, one very rich man to another, 'you *own* the Ritz.' He strolled on before I could deny it.

The pianist was playing Rex Harrison's song 'I've Grown Accustomed to Her Face' as I entered Spencer House a few hours after hearing of his death. He is released not only from cancer but also from near-blindness. When he opened in New York in *The Circle*, Marti Stevens sent him first-night flowers. When he rang to thank her he said: 'So kind, darling, I can't see the bloody things but they smell *marvellous*.' He had learnt the script of the play from a blown-up text with about one sentence per page.

A visiting English producer saw him during the out-of-town tour. 'How's Glynis?' he asked of Rex's co-star.

'Glynis who?'

'Glynis Johns.'

'Delightful girl,' said Rex. 'Haven't seen her for years.'

The best things about the Royal Academy's 221st dinner the same week were not the speeches – except the president's. Where Roger de Grey's was pithy and to the point, Julian Spalding, replying for the guests, and Richard Luce, responding to 'Her Majesty's Ministers', go to the bottom of the class. The Minister for the Arts actually trundled out 'in a world where the flame of freedom is burning ever more brightly...' with a straight face in one of several perorations interspersed with five false finishes and eighteen rambling sub-clauses. I was reminded of Beecham's judgement on Bruckner's inability to develop and organize a symphony. 'In the course of the first movement I took note of a dozen pregnancies – and half-a-dozen miscarriages.'

According to Kenneth Clark's book his father was often invited. Those were the days 'when elderly RAs traditionally interrupted the speeches of ministers of the Crown and ended up sliding off their chairs on to the floor.' Sadly they have lost the knack.

I didn't know that you could have pictures accepted by the Academy and not have them shown. The Duke of Buccleuch told me he had submitted three, of which two were accepted but not hung – the other, a still life, seems to have been lost. He pointed enviously to a picture by his cousin which was hung prominently. He said ruefully that he supposed he would have to buy it. He has and he loves it.

Consuming Passions

Reading Richard Huggett's biography, *Binkie Beaumont – Eminence Grise of the West End Theatre 1933–1973*, I was beguiled immediately by Mr Huggett's diligent research. Detailed conversations from long before the author was born are lovingly trotted out, and may well owe everything to old gentlemen with extraordinarily retentive memories; but Mr Huggett, who lives near the vegetable market in Berwick Street, is also obsessed by the food consumed by his impresario.

In 1923 Beaumont was helping to manage the Playhouse, Cardiff, and apparently he entertained tour stars royally at the Royal Hotel in 'the splendid and beautiful panelled room where Captain Scott had given his farewell banquet in 1911 before departing for the South Pole'. Binkie's discussion of suitable menus with the chef is said to have led to this piece of advice: 'How about a nice little bit of vichyssoise to start off with, Mr Beaumont? Really nice when it is chilled, you will see, and they'll love it ... or perhaps an avocado with prawns in a rich creamy sauce, and you could serve champagne with it – always a good start to a meal?'

Equipped with this knowledge some six years later when, in his early twenties, he was invited to lunch with the great Marie Tempest, 'he was able to show intelligent appreciation of her Royal Doulton dinner service and, in particular, the exquisite food which she served: smoked mackerel with lemon mayonnaise, chicken *à la Kiev*, and finally an orange and brandy sorbet'.

Now, I wondered, had Mr Huggett had access to the 1923 chef at the Royal, Cardiff, and to Dame Marie's cook in the early 1930s, or had he simply sat licking his lips in his perch over Old Compton Street imagining his favourite menus and feeding them to his subject?

It was the avocado which started my suspicions. We all know that Martin Fernandez de Enciso familiarized some Europeans with the avocado, and Jane Grigson tells us in her vegetable book that it was occasionally found in exceptional circumstances in England in the seventeenth century. Every schoolboy learns that George Sellon started cultivating avocados in Florida in the 1900s, but did it get as far as Cardiff, or Dame Marie's kitchen in the Avenue Road, in time for Mr Beaumont to spoon it off the Royal Doulton?

I know I didn't taste an avocado until the 1950s, but that proves nothing. With hindsight, the saddest day of my childhood must have been when we moved farms and my father pulled up the whole asparagus bed at the new place to make room for more utilitarian vegetables, and I didn't know what I was missing: but avocados were a closed cookery book to me.

I found an ally in my investigations in another senior impresario, Sir Peter Saunders, who exploded at the thought. 'Avocados in the Twenties? Nonsense!'

I considered the most cosmopolitan and sophisticated gourmet I could think of who would readily admit to dining out in the 1920s. Elisabeth Welch came instantly to mind. American by birth, Miss Welch never ate them on the West Side in New York when she was growing up or in Paris in the 1920s. In London, she first remembers seeing a few in the later 1930s in the windows of Solomon's, a long-gone exotic fruit and vegetable shop in the old arcade alongside the Ritz Hotel; but she didn't know what to do with them. She does now.

I called Keith Waterhouse, who has often boasted that his father was once known universally as the 'cucumber king of Leeds'. Pineapples they had in the 1930s, but no hint of an avocado. I remembered Russell Harty's proud claim that *his* father was 'the man who introduced the avocado to Blackburn' in the 1950s – twenty years on.

My Man in Deal reminded me of a famous spat before the war when Somerset Maugham, who was proud of his prowess as an avocado farmer at the Villa Mauresque, caught a greedy Cyril Connolly stealing one from the garden and considered not speaking to him again. But the whole point of that incident is that the avocado was rare, prized, exotic. Maugham would have forgiven a gooseberry.

I decided that more authoritative evidence was required. I spoke to Cyril Ray, who had recently poured some delicious Rizzardi wines down my gullet and at 81 is easily old enough to be authoritative. As usual in matters of food, he deferred to his wife. Liz Ray turned up a book by Morton Shand, *Fruit of the Tropics*, published in 1927, which hinted grudgingly that the avocado could be used in a salad but hardly recommended it.

She then unearthed *Don't Swallow the Avocado Pip*, a facetious American book published in the 1950s, which doesn't add much of interest to anyone save, perhaps, Simon Rattle: one Slim Galliard wrote his *Avocado Seed Soup Symphony* in America in the 1930s. I think it should be heard.

I tried Fortnum & Mason, who disowned any knowledge before the 1950s. The Savoy Hotel, now a hundred years old, searched its records and found no mention on the menus before the Second World War. 'Eddie the carver', who has been there for more than forty years, puts the début of the avocado at approximately 1954, chaperoned by a vinaigrette; prawns came later.

I remember when I was part of a consortium bidding for a breakfast television franchise that we were asked by the IBA if there was a demand for breakfast television. 'Was there a demand for the avocado before it arrived in the 1950s?' our spokesman asked. We did not get the franchise.

As if this was not conclusive evidence of Mr Huggett's fantasizing, I bumped into a long-time friend and colleague of Beaumont, Sir John Gielgud, at the BBC rehearsal rooms –

affectionately known as the Acton Hilton. I asked him about Huggett's avocado. He groaned. 'That's the least of the inaccuracies in the book,' he said.

Who knows more about Fortnum & Mason than Fortnum & Mason knows itself? Well, Dame Alicia Markova, for one. She had been continent hopping and got home from New York in time to read what I had researched before she flew back to Boston a few days later, but she called to tell me that although she has no knowledge of avocado supplies in Cardiff in the Twenties, back in 1919, when she was eight going on nine, her father, who had previously travelled to America, used to bring home (from Fortnum & Mason) grapefruit, Post Toasties (exotic early cornflakes) and alligator pears, as avocados were called then, because of their rough, crinkly skin.

Richard Huggett himself added some valuable information on the great avocado mystery. 'Every schoolboy knows that Mrs Patrick Campbell was eating avocados in 1914 while rehearsing for *Pygmalion*, but in those days they were known as prickly pears. Avocados were not widely eaten in the Twenties: they were a rare and horribly expensive delicacy, which is why none of Mr Sherrin's witnesses know about them. But my father remembers eating one at the Carlton Grill in 1921 when he took my mother there for an engagement dinner. Ironically, neither of them liked it and they never ate it again.

'Sorry, dear Ned, you've got it all wrong. But I forgive you.'

Not a word about avocados in Cardiff, I'm afraid.

One of my minor ambitions had always been to write the phrase 'This correspondence is now closed' and I proposed to invoke it for the Great Avocado Mystery. Subsequent to Esmée Connell's testimony in *The Times* letters column, Arthur Hill reported that he first encountered avocados in Bali in 1937 where Lord Tredegar insisted on one every day for his breakfast. Malcolm Duncan referred me to Ambrose Heath's *Good Food*, published in 1932, which recommends them for consumption in May '. . . . the empire month when, to reinforce

our scanty list, come the empire fruits ... granadillas and
avocado pears'.

June Pritchard's grandmother, who was born in Peru, used
to call them 'Paltas' and would ripen hers by 'wrapping them
in her combinations and keeping them in the airing cupboard'.
Mrs B Parry, who married an 'oilyboy' (lovely period phrase),
and went to live in Bogotá in 1939, learnt to mash them up
with a dressing.

Finally, Dr R E Jones started a whole new hare. 'Whoever
ate smoked or any other kind of mackerel before the war? This
fish was regarded as a scavenger and barely edible. Only with
the exhaustion of fish stocks in recent years has it come into
prominence.'

So much for ambitions. Remember, the question was *not*,
when did the avocado come to England? There is plenty of
evidence of that. John Sherns wrote from the South of France
that at Christmas 1931 you could get an avocado for a shilling
at his shop in the Tottenham Court Road. Now a hi-fi store,
I shouldn't wonder.

Donald Hickling quoted Cyril Connolly in 1936: 'Yquem
and avocado pears – a simple meal – but lots and lots of both.'
Revolting! Mr Wilkin of Hove speculated: 'Ciro of Monte
Carlo had a refrigerator van that went by rail with Scotch beef
and salmon and Southdown lamb. It seems improbable that
it went back empty.' He urged me to examine the records of
the Blue Train and Mrs Ronald Greville's menus at Polesdon
Lacy. Elizabeth David referred me to Sir Francis Colchester
Wemyss, who recommends avocado as 'the ideal salad to
go with pressed beef'. Elizabeth also wickedly suggests that
'notions of filling them with prawns, making them into a
mousse with eggs and so on, were aberrations of the 50s and
60s, the sort of thing one found in Chelsea and Belgravia
restaurants ... I'm not sure that the recipes weren't put about
by the avocado growers themselves.'

No, the question was, were they likely to have been served
with prawns to the impresario Binkie Beaumont in Cardiff in
1921, and was the avocado ever called a prickly pear? Cyril

Ray, no respecter of persons, attacked Richard Huggett's late parents. They introduced the heresy of calling avocados prickly pears. 'If the avocado pear was known in 1921 as a prickly pear, it shouldn't have been. The prickly pear is the fruit of a cactus eaten in Mexico (where it is known as *tuna*), in Sicily (*bastardo* or *bastardone*) ... also known as the Barbary Fig.' Mrs Peck of Chichester and Hugh Pitt of Sherbourne also took the prickly pear bait. Both identify it as *Opuntia* or *Fighi d'India*. Mr Pitt claims the avocado as *Persea americana*, a member of the laurel family; 'it grows extensively in East Africa, and I knew a family near Nairobi who kept a large dog who barked vigorously beneath the tree (when ordered to do so), to bring off the fruit.' David Climie remembered them as alligator pears in the 60s, 'named thus because of their tough skins. By the same analogy,' he wrote, 'presumably you would call an overbaked cake a Crocodile Dundee!'

I print Richard Huggett's reply with no comment, but with a delicately raised eyebrow hinting at wisdom after the event.

'The chef told me that as a lad he had enjoyed a full training and apprenticeship at the Carlton in London ... when he got his job in Cardiff he brought with him all his knowledge of rare specialist foods to enliven the rather humdrum menus which the management forced on him and, if anything was difficult to obtain in Wales, he would send to the Carlton for them. Binkie's Saturday night dinners offered him virtually the only chance of showing what he could do, and he was very sorry when Binkie left the city.'

Huggett spent twelve years researching the book, so he must be congratulated on tracking down his man at least 56 years after he served the food. Compared to that, finding the chef who committed the smoked mackerel with a lemon mayonnaise to which Dame Marie Tempest treated Binkie only forty-odd years ago must have been a snip.

Now, about this mackerel (*Scomber scombros*, or *macarellus* in Medieval Latin). Dr R E Jones was the man who first harboured suspicions. 'I doubt if Marie Tempest served mackerel – a poorly regarded scavenger fish, with or without a lemon mayonnaise.' Ms David concedes that it is just possible; but hopes Dame Marie had better taste. It certainly wasn't a luxury in the thirties, she says, although it has a respectable history in Germany and the Low Countries. She rustled up an 1847 book by James Robinson, *18 Years a Practical Curer*, which admits it is 'much esteemed, particularly on the continent and by mariners'. My Man in Deal agreed to inquire of the fisher folk. One of them produced another book called *Anglers Evenings* (1890). Its author caught 25 dozen and refers to it as 'a rather monotonous kind of fishing'. I thought that was true of all fishing. Mackerel were marketed in Deal before the war by 'the long hundred'. May is the best month and they go off pretty damn quick. On the whole Deal was indifferent to the Great Mackerel Hunt, and keener on Deal sprats, a regular on the menu of the Lord Mayor's banquet before the First World War. (Were they the ones used to catch a mackerel?) And the excellent Deal dab, from which they believe we get the expression 'dab handed'.

It would all be small potatoes to Harold Ross, late editor of *The New Yorker*, who once rang his checking department to ask if Moby Dick was the man or the fish!

HARD ON MY resolution to get off the subject of food, I found myself bidding fair to succeed Lord Goodman to the nickname 'Two Dinners'; and as I realized that I was liable to usurp his title, so I began to speculate on the origin of the good lord's famous sobriquet.

Surely it must go back more than the thirty-odd years of the life of *Private Eye* magazine? Is there not an age of excess which proclaimed the first holder of the title? A Roman 'Two Dinners Tiberius', perhaps, or some other emperor with fingers so fat that he used his wife's necklaces as rings; or an eighteenth-century 'Two Dinners Tunbelly Clumsy'?

I fled to Brillat-Savarin, a good port in any foody storm, and thought I might have scored a direct hit on the first page of his preface. He writes, albeit in a footnote, '"Come and dine with me next Thursday," Ms de Greffulhe said to me one day, "I will arrange a dinner with scientists or men of letters, whichever you prefer."

'"My choice is made," I replied: "We will dine twice." Which we did, and the meal with the men of letters was noticeably the choicer and more delicate of the two.'

But there was no Richard Ingrams around to tag him 'Two Dinners Brillat-Savarin'.

Admitting defeat I rang Ingrams, or rather I rang Mrs Ingrams, the sage being in the country where there is no telephone. She was quite sure that the phrase had been new minted by her man. It all started when the Rhodesian sanctions talks were going on between Harold Wilson and Ian Smith.

One night Wilson and Goodman, who was advising him, dined on the *Tiger*. An urgent message arrived from Smith. Would not Wilson come for more talks over dinner? 'But I've already had dinner,' was Wilson's reaction. Not so Lord Goodman's. His inclination was to lower himself immediately into launch and limo and continue discussions while consuming a second repast; and so the legend of 'Two Dinners Goodman' was born.

But why am I challenging the distinguished holder of the title? Not because, as the junior subaltern responsible for catering in a Royal Signals mess in Beethoven Strasse, Klagenfurt, Austria, in 1950, I once ordered a meal so disgusting that my fellow officers insisted that we drive into town and eat another in the Landhauskeller at my expense.

No, it was a much more recent event. I have spoken a couple of times at 'Men of the Year' luncheons, impressive events organized by the Royal Association for Disability and Rehabilitation to recognize courage, heroism, imagination and energy in men. These lunches are presided over by Viscount Tonypandy, George Thomas to you and me, who was himself Man of the Year when he retired as Speaker in 1983.

These lunches have been going on for thirty years now, and an idea was introduced that previous award-winners should have a get-together once a year in a warm mood of reunion, reflection and fellowship. I assumed it was a lunch. A few weeks earlier I got a call from Peter Boizot, who runs the Pizza Express chain, which includes one of the few good remaining cabaret rooms in London, the Pizza on the Park, oddly situated by the side of the National Farmers Union building near Hyde Park Corner, but home to great jazz artists and unique cabaret performers like Blossom Dearie and Peter Greenwell. A dark side of Boizot and Pizza Express, of which I had not known, is that he also sponsors the London Hockey League. I became aware when he asked me to speak at their annual dinner and prize-giving at the Café Royal on a Tuesday night. 'Nothing easier,' I said, 'I'm doing the Men of the Year lunch, but there's nothing happening in the evening.'

On Monday I got a puzzled call from Lucy Green, the Men of the Year organizer. An Olympic hockey player, Veryan Pappin (the entire team were Men of the Year last year), had asked who was speaking; when told that I was he seemed surprised, because, he said, I was also talking to the London Hockey League. 'Are you coming to us?' Lucy asked plaintively. I checked the information she had sent me and plainly it was for dinner. It was all my fault.

Fortunately the Men of the Year dos are run with military precision, and the hockey players are a convivial lot, so I was able to enjoy *la Petite Salade de Volaille Fumée Croquante* and *Le Petit Tournedos de Boeuf aux Echalottes* at the Savoy. I passed on *le Mélange de Soufflé Glacé et Sorbet Marie Brizard* in favour of cheese. I was reminded of Winston Churchill, who once rejected a dessert at 10 Downing Street, grandly saying: 'This pudding has no theme.' Theme puddings indeed! We'll be having designer puddings before we know where we are. After the cheese I did my bit and nipped across to Regent Street to share the remains of the pea soup and bread and butter pudding with Sean Kerly and the rest of the Olympic team and the London Hockey League.

Two Dinners Sherrin at last.

Grace is traditionally said on these occasions by the Very Reverend Lawrence Jackson, Provost of Blackburn, who had been on parade at the Savoy already that day for a lunch for the blind. A few nights ago he had dinner with the Bishop of Durham, and at the end of the evening tried to press him to a large brandy. 'Oh, no, Lawrence,' said the bishop, 'if I had any more alcohol I might say something indiscreet.' Now, here's another point for anecdote authenticators. I re-told that story to a woman at the dinner, who swore that Lawrence had told it to her but gave the bishop's line as, 'Oh, no, I might say something *discreet*.' Jackson says 'indiscreet' is the correct text; but both are funny. I go along with 'indiscreet', which has a true ring of holy innocence about it which is exactly in character.

As a GENUINE son of the soil, I felt obliged to turn out for the Festival of British Food and Farming in Hyde Park. My resolve was strengthened by an invitation to enjoy the Great British Breakfast in the Weetabix marquee. In return for breakfast, I had to read out the winners of the LBC competition for children to make as many words as they could out of the letters in 'Great British Breakfast'. Miss Maria Carim (aged 11 years, four months) won with 1,089, and was quite shameless in her use of plurals to up the numbers. A bright little boy, who spoke only Bengali until last October, was a deserving runner-up. The more imaginative challenge was for children to describe a breakfast a hundred years hence. Miss Ganicka Martin (aged eight) reckons we shall all be living under water and varying a diet of pills with 'sea walnut muesli with skimmed sea cow milk, followed by laver bread toast with sea gooseberry jam, washed down with kelp tea'.

John Selwyn Gummer, the Minister of Agriculture, gave a short, businesslike address. Did you know that when Robert Walpole was Prime Minister he used to open letters from his farm bailiff before turning to government correspondence? I can't see Mrs Thatcher turning to Selwyn Gummer's missives first at 10 Downing Street. When I left the tent to inspect the rest of the showground, I began to get a picture of the farming community which was very different from the one I remember in Somerset. Judging by the most prominently displayed exhibits, the staples of our agriculture these days are oysters, ice-cream and English wine. I know Alcuin wrote home from France in the ninth century to say how much he missed 'the good wines of England', but it was news to me that they were so important today. I resisted a temptation to buy a 'Pig Lib' T-shirt, or to wear an 'I Love Wales' sticker, even though farmers are up against it in Wales these days.

I ignored the British Butterfly and Conservation Society and a display of organic haggis. In the Wessex tent someone in the Dorset section wanted a blackboard. 'Don't worry,' said his colleague. 'We can borrow one from Somerset.'

Somerset was selling *The Collected Poems of John Osborne*, already in its fourth reprint and including one specially written for the show.

> 'British food and farming
> has always been the best
> the products of our industry
> have always stood the test.'

I thought £2.50 was a snip for this rare edition of verses by one of our leading playwrights, especially as Herbert Kretzmer reminded me recently that when Osborne was writing his musical, *The World of Paul Slickey*, he told Kretzmer: 'Writing lyrics is like writing bad poetry – it's not easy.' You can say that again. He certainly gave poor Janet Hamilton-Smith an impossible exit in that show, rhyming 'horse and carriages' with 'Claridges', which Christopher Whelan set on a particularly high note. You try singing 'Clar-I-Dges' and ending well up the scale. Unfortunately, having paid my money and settled down to enjoy John's poems, I came across a picture of the author leaning on a cow by a farmyard gate – and not remotely resembling the apostle of anger. John Osborne (poet and farmer) might care to study Stephen Duck's 1,736 lines in 'The Thresher's Labour', which he can find in the *Penguin Book of English Pastoral Verse* (though come to think of it, he is about to find it here):

'But when the scorching sun is mounted high,
And no kind barns with friendly shade are nigh:
Our weary scythes entangle in the grass'
(here Duck's rhyming courage fails him)
'While streams of sweat run trickling down ... a pace'.

A pen of sheep was the biggest attraction for crowds of kids who had never seen a sheep before. It is the sort of ignorance that tripped up a London-based company in the 1930s, when it acquired an Australian sheep station. The price of wool rose sharply, and head office sent a cable saying: 'Start shearing.' The immediate reply was: 'Cannot shear. Lambing.' Management cabled their informed response: 'Stop lambing start shearing.'

When I was directing the old 'Tonight' television programme, I went home one weekend and found myself moving my father's sheep along a quiet country road. A car pulled up behind me, and a man with a clipboard got out and asked what was my favourite television show. Putting on the thickest Somerset accent I could manage I said: '"Tonight".' He seemed pleased. He wrote it down and asked what I particularly liked about the programme. 'The quality of the direction,' I said, hoping to do myself a bit of good. But at that point he rumbled me and left me to my muttons.

Sheep farming founded the first great personal fortunes made in England from trade. Not for nothing does the Lord Chancellor sit on a Woolsack. Donald Baverstock saved Norman St John Stevas (as he then was) from some embarrassment when he was appearing on 'Tonight' to comment on Lord Dilhorne's elevation to the Woolsack. Norman had it in mind to say that this was the first time we had had a Woolsack on the Woolsack, which was accurate and funny but wouldn't have helped him much in his political advancement.

Enough farming, I thought, and since the Great British Breakfast, the fresh air and the sight of all those oysters and ice-cream had given me an appetite, I decided to take nice Mr Gardhouse, who produces 'Loose Ends', to Nico Ladenis's new restaurant, Chez Nico, which is near the BBC in Great Portland Street. Actually I didn't decide it there and then, because the place is already booked out weeks ahead; but I was very glad I had made provision. I needed Gardhouse for a little plot I was hatching as much as for his fund of good stories and his skill as a listener. Some time ago Marmaduke Hussey, the chairman of the BBC Board of Governors, told me of his dismay that Nico was moving premises from Rochester Row (to which Hussey used regularly to stray). Now, with the restaurant on his own doorstep, he was worried that he would be self-consciously surrounded by senior BBC employees, whose expense accounts he would later have to countersign.

The restaurant, elegant and airy, was jam-packed, and I set Gardhouse to work to identify all the hungry BBC staff. I was planning a head-count; but unfortunately we couldn't find a single BBC person. Concealing our disappointment, we demolished the delicate langouste consommé, the melting liver in a mustardy sauce and the lavish selection of sorbets. At least I spotted the perfect table for Hussey: it is for two, just inside the door, and an ideal place for him to autograph BBC expense accounts as his executives reel out.

HAVING INTENDED TO keep off the subject of food for a while I came across a phenomenon. We went to Orso (is it the only restaurant named after a dead dog?) My guest was Gerald Asher, a trail-blazing wine importer in the 50s and now a busy and witty wine writer and consultant in California. Gerald it was who introduced most of London to *Muscat Beaune de Venise* partly by lodging a bottle in Elizabeth David's early-morning milk basket one day when she was ill. He hastened her recovery no end. Sins have been committed in its name since then but it did a lot for dessert wines. I cherish his comment on the autobiography of Craig Claiborne, the star cookery writer of *The New York Times*: 'He describes, I am told, seduction by his father, with whom he had an affair. The trouble with dishing up a story like that in Chapter One, when the final chapter deals with your new salt-free diet, is that if the end and the beginning are tasteless, who can be sure about the middle?'

Anyway, with all these credentials he couldn't help me much on the Orso revolution – which was black pasta. *Black pasta!* Pasta white as the driven, came (I had always heard) from China, courtesy of Marco Polo; so maybe Richard Polo who runs Orso was trying to improve on his famous namesake-ancestor. But then I found Marco and his claim to be the father of pasta is a grey area. The Chinese had noodles at least as early as the first century AD. *Nudel* is a German word. One early Chinese writer commented that although the common people invented noodles it was the foreigner who taught them the best way to prepare them. There is a lot of evidence that India and the Middle East were into noodles by AD 1200 (M Polo 1256–1323). Poets, among them Iacopone da Todi who died in 1306, were writing boring poems such as *Per virtu la lasagne* and Boccaccio told of 'a mountain made entirely of grated Parmesan cheese on which people lived who did nothing but make macaroni and ravioli'.

Leaping forward to the eighteenth century, we get the industrial pasta revolution with the first pasta machines in Naples; a hundred years later Marinetti, the Futurist writer, was blaming these pale, farinaceous strips for 'the weakness, pessimism, inactivity, nostalgia and neutralism of my countrymen'. Most of it is white, so whence this black pasta craze? Florence Fabricant has been researching the same subject for the *New York Times*. The chef at the Everest Room in Chicago learnt to make black pasta and, of course, risotto in Venice. Rice, coloured black with the ink of squid or cuttlefish, is a commonplace in parts of Italy and Spain. At the River Café in Brooklyn they make black couscous, using black olive paste as a colouring agent.

Why is black suddenly so beautiful? Fabricant quotes the answer: designer food. 'Black edibles are now held in high esteem ... Black has more drama; the customer reacts positively to black because it has an upscale professional feel.'

Black rice, black pasta, black mushrooms, black truffles, black olives, black beans and *nori* (a black Japanese seaweed) are running riot in New York, as well as blackened Cajun food and gleaming decorations of black caviare. At a club in Washington black pasta is called 'Midnight Noodles'. What is more you can buy black pasta and cook it at home.

In a desperate attempt to keep up with the black-Joneses I have just had lunch: black olives, black pudding and black grapes on sparkling white plates. Goodness, I feel up-scale professionally, but then any excuse for black pudding is welcome.

THE CHUTNEY CONNECTION turned me on to another charming little footnote to gastronomic history. Denis Healey and I were talking to colleagues and clients of Sharwoods, the spice people, who were celebrating the centenary of the firm at Simpsons in the Strand. Old James Allen Sharwood's life started romantically and ended in black farce. Opening a wine department in a grocer's shop, he expanded by shipping 'French comestibles' to the Viceroy of India. Lord Dufferin's French chef introduced him to oriental spices and he shipped them back to England. He went solo in 1889, and retired in

1927. For the rest of his life he travelled the world, always accompanied by an embalming kit because he didn't trust foreign undertakers. He died in South Africa in 1939, and not before the early 1950s could his wish to be buried beside his wife in Wimbledon be honoured. By now the embalming kit was forgotten and his ashes were shipped to Southampton. *En route* to Wimbledon the lorry was hijacked and presumably the villains, finding no use for his ashes, scattered them in the Hampshire hedgerows. So somewhere in that rich earth there lies a richer dust concealed, a dust which gave us curry powder, chutney, Bombay ducks, Chinese figs and poppadums, and is forever Sharwoods.

ONCE I BREAKFASTED on alligator. I met my 'alligator creole style' at the new Billingsgate along with marinated, soft-shelled crawfish on toast, cajun kedgeree, crawfish mousse, and tuna *matelotte*. I had never visited the old fish market, and an invitation from my local wet fishmongers, R W Larkins, sparked my curiosity. Older than Smithfield, Spitalfields and Leadenhall, it is mentioned by Ethelred in 979. Centuries on, Shakespeare nicked his plot for *King Lear* from an indifferent drama which spelt the King's name 'Leir'. In it the inevitable messenger boasts: 'As bad a tongue as any oyster wife at Billingsgate.' It was about then that the market began to concentrate on fish.

I can confirm that the tradition of lively *badinage* from the porters survives. In the seventeenth century, Nicholas Culpeper referred to 'downright Billingsgate rhetoric'. In 1760 a Billingsgate was a 'scolding impudent slut', and a hundred years later one chap was said to be 'no better than a Billingsgate fish-fag'.

I turned up for a 7.30am tour of the market, carrying my Gladstone bag without which I rarely move. The porters no longer wear the wood and leather 'bobbing hats' which were said to be little changed versions of the helmets of English archers at Agincourt – I hope Kenneth Branagh has them right in *Henry V*. But they greeted my bag with jocular cries of:

'Here comes Dr Crippen ... Dr Death ... Dr Foster went to Gloucester', and: 'Fred, Fred – that baby you've ordered's arrived.' The uncooked fish were a multicoloured mixture of huge turbots, humble herrings, emperor prawns, groupers, and all their newly fashionable fellows. The breakfast buffet was heavily spiced with Tabasco.

Sylvain Ho Wing-Cheong of Chez Liline ('one of London's foremost fish chefs') had sprinkled the McIlhenny inheritance prodigally. Canny readers will have gleaned by now that I was at a Tabasco promotion.

Those Mexican chillies were first imported to Avery Island, Louisiana, in 1868 by a soldier returning from the Mexican wars, fifty years after the McIlhenny family had settled there. Tabasco remains an exclusive family business and a highly profitable one. The word translates as 'damp earth'. It refers to the fertile ground in which the Mexican peppers grew. Oddly this was the place where our old friend 'Stout' Cortez first landed on his way to defeat Montezuma. The way is now clear for Peter Shaffer to start on *The Royal Hunt of the Sauce*. I liked the crawfish mousse best. The Tabasco people told me that their product is addictive – so look out for Tabasco-House parties with hot music any day now.

REFLECTING ON THE German problem, I must sound a note of caution before we all become too fearfully Germanophile. Not surprisingly, it's about food. President Kennedy started it when he gallantly proclaimed: '*Ich bin ein Berliner*', literally claiming that he was a doughnut. Imagine if he had been speaking in Frankfurt or Hamburg or, worse still, in the Black Forest with its appalling gâteau (popular myth has it that the man who invented portion control has a stately home in the North of England which he has christened Black Forest Château). Are we now to be flooded with Bismarck herrings, Battenburg cake, Carlsbad plums and even more lager for the louts? Tear down the wall, certainly, but please keep an eye open for the sauerkrauts.

BACK IN THE 60s everybody had to have a boutique. In the 70s you had to have a personal money crisis. In the 80s it was a column in a newspaper. Then in the 90s, it seemed everyone had to have a restaurant. Early in the decade the actress Susan George opened hers, Willows, English country house décor, Mediterranean cuisine, near the barracks in Knightsbridge on the site of the old Wellington Club.

However, the old guard fight back. I had lunch at a packed Scotts. It is 21 years since the Kermans moved from Coventry Street and they plan a series of coming-of-age parties, but first I collected a splendid 'overheard' from the next table. An American looked at the prices and visibly blanched. I saw his eye travel down the menu to the cheapest dish – liver and bacon. Seeking to save face in this temple of fish, he launched into his order: 'I hear you are famous for your liver and bacon . . .'

IT'S ODD WHAT a duff tooth and tongue do for your diet – even mine. Living out of a suitcase and looking for easily swallowable food during rehearsals of *Same Old Moon* in Southampton, I found my habitual healthy diet was hurled into confusion. At the Nuffield Theatre I sampled various dishes named in honour of our play. Vatican Taramasalata, Galway Bay Fish Pie and Café Daphne's celery and cashew nut risotto slipped down fairly easily. In the University's John Arlott bar I enriched the soup of the day five days running by spricing it liberally with dry sherry in homage to the man whom the bar honours. I also sampled his 'prawn fantasie' (prawns in a bun). British Rail offered InterCity croissants, Peak Frean's large traditional Cornish pastie and a beef casserole which I was persuaded to eat instead of their chicken dish by a buffet attendant with the throwaway line, 'My middle name is George, I cannot tell a lie.' Late one night I hoped to celebrate a highly successful preview with my annual helping of fish and chips. Unfortunately 'Big George' – open till midnight – was, at 11.50pm, serving only doner kebabs. However, the obliging man at Portswood Fish and Chip and Chinese Takeaway just up the road abandoned his kung fu video and fried some splendid cod which made it all worthwhile.

IF YOU ARE planning a weekend in Budapest, you should check the restaurants with the King's Singers before you set out. They happened upon one behind the Opera. An unimposing entrance gave on to an Aladdin's cave of chandeliers and crystal plate, called the Baroque. The bill for four totalled only £30. They had a choice of Mete Gele ('trembling jellied meat'), Miscued Poullet Salade, Ice-cooled Spawn, Cow meat suddenly Roasted with Salsa, Lifer of Gose in Aristocratic style, and Vegetarian Eatables to the liking of the Hermit. That was for starters.

'Our chief dishes' included *Iointe* (pork) rosted in one block with Villein's Lumplings, That Caboche with Mete for the Capuchin Munuc, Knokel of Pigge for the Toth of Konigsberg and Eatable Grudinovich in Salsa with Ginger. Occasionally we reach recognizable landmarks – The Favourite Pilau of Stroganoff, Tournedos according to the taste of Rossini and Disc of Markis Chateaubriand with a Heap of Vegetables.

THERE WAS A 'Taste of the 90s Luncheon' at Claridges to celebrate Scottish salmon. Somehow, 'the King of freshwater fish' failed to rise in two pedestrian recipes – souffléd with a spinach coulis or baked, smothered by a warm vinaigrette. 'It wasn't the wine,' murmured Mr Snodgrass in a broken voice (in *Pickwick Papers*). 'It was the salmon.' I am with Mr Snodgrass.

Then there was the Sunday wake for Peter Langan, who would have been 49. Langan's was stuffed with survivors – George Best, Henry Cooper, both Ronnies, Bob Hoskins, Ben Kingsley and all. Keith Waterhouse suggested two minutes' hubbub, pulling girls screaming under tables, instead of the more usual two minutes' silence. He was not heeded. Langan

already has two biographers. Brian Sewell's book was on
display. Christopher Wilson, 'the official biographer', said
Sewell had declined to assist him as he was being paid. He
wondered if Sewell was accepting royalties? He didn't know
(few did, did you?) that Langan's house was filmed by Loyd
Grossman for 'Through the Keyhole' a few days before his
death and so was never used – macabre footage for a TV
obituary? The journalist Mike Molloy thought it would have
been the party to set the new decade if only Jeffrey Archer had
been there. Molloy was in Grantchester for the Archer bash
after his ultra-fragrant libel case. Curious to find out what
happened in a folly at the bottom of the garden, he and Clive
James peered in. There, unattended, was a word processor
spookily tapping out an Archer novel.

At Cliveden, to which I haven't been since Alan Brien had
a cottage there in Keeler days, we launched the Ackerman/
Martell *Food and Hotel Guide*. Lunch was a good deal jollier
than the weekend Bob Boothby and Harold Nicolson spent
there in November 1930. Boothby recorded a 'glass of white
wine was all you got … the Oswald Mosleys brought a
petrol tin to my room. It was filled with martini.' Nicolson
added: 'After dinner to enliven the party Lady Astor dons a
Victorian hat and a pair of false teeth. It does *not* enliven the
party.' On our visit scandalized foodies, tongues loosened by
liquids, fed me accounts of the meal my splendid colleague
Clement Freud cooked at 190 Queensgate a few weeks ago.
The exotic menu read, 'Soup (white wine), Fish, Meat (red
wine), Pud (more wine).' The new Escoffier's soup was
Campbell's consommé (excellent for Bullshots) and his fish
was cakes. Why were details of this culinary triumph not more
readily forthcoming?

Then the South Bank Centre hosted a day of music – inside,
outside, up and down the foyers, on boats. It climaxed with a
Simon Rattle gala, all to raise cash for Aids relief and support.
They asked me to do a programme note about brunch – there
was a brunch/cabaret at noon. I had always assumed that
brunch was an American invention – maybe it is; but there is

a reference to it in *Punch* back in August 1896. 'To be fashionable nowadays we must "brunch", truly an excellent port-
manteau word introduced last year by Mr Guy Beringer in the
now defunct *Hunters' Weekly*, and indicating a combined
breakfast and lunch.' The next year the *Westminster Gazette*
escalated the word into verse:

> Perish scrambling breakfast, formal lunch!
> Hardened night birds fondly cherish
> All the subtle charms of *brunch*.

WOULD YOU CREDIT it? Recently judges and restaurateurs have
banded together in an unholy alliance. The restaurateurs complained of customers who booked tables in their restaurants
and then didn't turn up. The judges have held that in these
cases mine host or mine hostess or mine hostperson, can, if he
or she has been clever enough to get the customer's credit card
number, charge for the meal which the customer didn't turn
up to eat. This worried my friend, Neil Shand, and me no end.

How do they know what food we are going to order? Not,
we hasten to add, that we are the sort of people who would
ever book a table and not show. Mr Shand is definitely an
escargot de saumon fumé mousseline aux herbes person whereas
Mr Sherrin can invariably be found behind a plate of *rosette de
veaux aux nouilles et son endive au jambon* which, as everybody
knows, is a nugget of veal lightly pan fried, coated in morel
sauce and a cordon of veal jus with a spaghetti of carrot gratin
dauphinoise, and chicory wrapped in Parma ham braised in
veal jus. This he is in the habit of ordering with a mug of tea
and two slices of white bread and butter.

How do they know what we are going to drink? How do
they know how many bottles of Perrier (the 1958 vintage from
the north side of the spring) Mr Shand will consume? Are they
wise to the fact that though Mr Sherrin's heart may be in
Latour his wallet floats in the house red. What about *digestifs*?
How many coffee beans set alight on top of a sambucca makes

five? How long is a piece of string bean? How deep is the ocean? How green was my valley?

And can one be sure that when they submit their reckoning to American Access (Never leave home without your flexible friend) they won't have added fifteen per cent for service. ('I do hope everything was all right, sir?')

On the other hand, what happens if Sir Cyril Smith, Sir Clement Freud and Giant Haystacks turn up at the restaurant and are given our table in our absence. Ignoring for a moment the impertinence of this – after all, we received no phone call asking if it was all right if they took our table – let us consider what they ate – actually, consumed would be a better word. Sir Cyril went for *côte d'agneau pöelé et sa compote de legumes* (just before it went for him), Sir Clement downed *délice de saumon aux écailles de courgette et St Jacques provençale* and chips and Giant Haystacks went into the ring with the *salade de rougets de roche pöelés à l'huile de homard*, tucked into a hearty *crepinette de ris de veau aux épinards au salpicon de crustace, ris sauvage*, polished off the *chartreuse de volaille de Bresse et foie gras de canard aux choux* and then got three falls and a submission. Reach for your calculators. We're talking Big Bills here, and we don't mean large policemen. We have to pay when all we did was to stay at home and nibble on a bit of dry toast. Never mind taking us to court. They should be paying us and looking forward to the time when we ring again to book a table which we won't be using.

This unfortunate precedent will plainly lead to all restaurateurs demanding your credit card number when you make a reservation. Why not give the number of a friend, or better still an enemy? Preferably an enemy who drinks and won't be able to remember whether he went to the restaurant or not.

Mind you, we can see advantages in this new legal development – if it is extrapolated beyond the world of catering.

Who would not pay dearly to miss Michael Winner's next movie? Mr Madvah Sharma for one.

Who would surrender their credit card to avoid an evening of gentle, tasteful humour with Mr Bernard Manning?

Who would not phone all their numbers to Our Price to avoid having to listen to Mr Rick Astley's latest trip down the Middle of the Road?

See you at the Caprice, corner table, 8 for 8.30. If you get there at nine and see Sir Cyril Smith, Sir Clement Freud, Giant Haystacks and Judge Michael Argyll pigging it you'll know we didn't turn up.

Two old waiter jokes revisited:

Customer: Waiter, waiter, what is this fly doing in my soup?

Waiter: The breast stroke, sir.

Same customer: Waiter, waiter, there's a fly in my soup.

Different waiter: Yes, sir, the chef used to be a tailor.

Curtain Up

One of the best things about being drawn into the camaraderie of a television studio is the amount of theatrical gossip it yields.

Where else would I have got paid to have lunch with someone who told me that there was a new *Wuthering Heights* musical looming and that Cliff Richard was keen to embody the animal magnetism of Heathcliff? Kylie Minogue for Cathy? Or that most of the Glyndebourne cast of *Porgy and Bess* played it before in Houston and New York and since in San Francisco, and now refer to this regular meal ticket as *Porgy and Beans*? Or that 'Don't Cry For Me Argentina' from *Evita*, started life with a first line 'I couldn't love you for ever'; and was only changed after the initial recording because it didn't have much to do with Peronist politics in Buenos Aires, so a new first line was dropped in. Apparently, really clever collectors have copies of the original. Or that Trevor Nunn auditioned an actress and singer, Rebecca Storme, for *Aspects of Love* and said: 'No! No! But you'd be perfect as Fantine in my production of *Les Misérables*,' to which she replied: 'I am now playing Fantine in your production of *Les Misérables*.' I worry a bit about this one, which smacks of the old tale of a Grade or some other agent saying excitedly 'Who represents you?' to a conjuring act who replies: 'You did – until tonight.' (*see End Notes*)

My favourite Trevor Nunn story is the true one of a band of RSC actors who wrote to Jimmy Savile when Nunn was artistic director of the company, and asked if Jim could fix it for them to meet him. Another joyful bonus in these circumstances is the average performer's total lack of information about the creators whom they interpret. Howard Goodall, who composed the *Marguerita* parody for the BBC's ten years of Thatcher show, has two West End musicals to his credit, the highly regarded *A Hired Man* and the less highly regarded *Girlfriends*. He was approached by an enthusiastic singer who asked him if he had ever thought of writing a whole West End show. He extricated himself with dignity.

I once received a letter which showed a matching blissful ignorance. The writer asked for an autograph and wished me the best as the director of Victor Spinetti's very successful *Very Private Diary* which had just reopened at the Apollo Theatre. The letter gave the game away. 'I do hope the show goes well,' he continued, 'if you are as good a director as you are an actor I'm sure it will be a smash hit!' As my entire professional experience as an actor consists of two minutes playing Noël Coward opposite the late Alan Badel on television in 1975, the success of *Very Private Diary* had to depend entirely on Spinetti, which was just as well.

I WAS STARTING on yet another book of theatre anecdotes (any suggestions for snappy titles and new stories would have been welcome). But staying at Hickstead Place over Easter highlighted one of the problems.

John Hurt, a fellow guest, was in fine anecdotal form; but how many versions are there of that story about 'Wait till you see Buckingham'? For the uninitiated: two actors reel on stage at the beginning of *Richard III*, after a very liquid lunch, and are accused by a voice from the gallery of being drunk. 'Wait,' one replies defiantly, 'until you see the Duke of Buckingham.' It is usually ascribed to the late great Wilfred Lawson; but was anybody there?

Sometimes the attributions are downright unfair. Noël Coward, in spite of popular belief, did not write every extra stanza for 'Eskimo Nell', and poor Sarah Miles was not the principal in another story evoked again that weekend. It may be apocryphal, but the star is Sylvia Miles. Who is Sylvia (Miles), what is she? This is of course the reason for the confusion. She is a distinguished American actress (*Midnight Cowboy* on film and *Vieux Carré* here at the Piccadilly Theatre on stage).

Victor Spinetti immortalized her in his recent show for walking down a street in New York with Tennessee Williams, who spotted an alarmingly thin woman on the opposite side-walk. 'She's so *thin*!' he exclaimed. 'Oh, Tennessee,' said Miles, 'that's anorexia nervosa.' 'Oh, Sylvia,' said Tennessee. 'You know everyone!'

But the tale I had to correct at Hickstead was of Miles's aborted passion for a homosexual. I repeat it may or may not be apocryphal. When the lad abandoned her, she sought solace in the bottle at Joe Allen's restaurant. One night, a black waiter suggested coffee to sober her up. 'How do you like your coffee, Ms Miles?' he enquired. She looked him up and down and fell back on a cliché: 'Like my men.' His voice went up a register. 'Sorry, Ms Miles, we don't serve no gay coffee here.' And poor Sarah Miles, doubtless a few thousand miles away at the time, has had to live with it.

Of course it isn't only the theatre which cannot keep control of its anecdotes. Douglas Bunn, the master of Hickstead, unearthed the legal chestnut about the absent-minded pro-fessor of law (at Cambridge, he said) who met a graduate long gone down and asked: 'Now tell me, my boy, was it you or your brother who was killed during the war?' I have always heard that attributed to the Vinerian professor of law at Oxford who said it in the Turl – it is these bewitching little bits of local colour that make you think you've got it right.

One of the risks of anecdoting at Hickstead is that if the story takes Mrs Bunn's fancy she is inclined to make you repeat it several times during the weekend, with diminishing reactions from the other guests. She also tells very good jokes herself, none of which can be repeated in print.

I went to the Old Vic the following Tuesday for the first night of the Eric Porter-Jonathan Miller *King Lear*, and very moving it was. Miller has said somewhere that he has now done five *Lears*, one for each of his last five decades, and that this is his middle-aged essay (I would love to have seen his eleven-year-old version), but the mention of middle age always sends me scuttering back into nostalgia.

My first Lear was William Devlin's at the Bristol Old Vic just after the war. Meriel Moore and Rosalie Crutchley were the wicked sisters. A strapping Robert Eddison was Edmund and the elderly Leon Quartermaine was Kent. Some years later I paid my first visit to the Haymarket Theatre and sat in the gallery for *A Day By the Sea*. I helped an old lady open her bottle of smelling salts and struck up an acquaintance. (Murderers have started off as easily.) 'Ah,' she cooed, 'such a pretty theatre. I saw *Mary Rose* here with little Fay Compton and young Leon Quartermaine.'

One of the strong pillars of the Porter-Miller *Lear* was Paul Rogers as Gloucester. He was my first Tybalt in *Romeo* at Bristol. John Byron was Romeo, Jane Wenham was Juliet and Nigel Stock Mercutio, Daniel Day Lewis's mother, Jill Balcon, was an improbably young Lady Capulet. Nostalgia ricochets on. There was Robert Eddison's Hamlet. At school we were reading a bodice-ripper called *Cue for Passion* with one really purple passage. When Eddison came to the line: 'The motive and the cue for passion', a whole row of callow schoolboys fell about. I have always wondered if Robert tried to get the laugh back the next night. To make the evening more memorable, Gertrude's left breast popped out at one point, which was a great embellishment on Shakespeare.

Eric Porter's first fine Lear was at Bristol. It is another disputed story. Peter O'Toole, who was in it, confirmed to me the other day that at notes at the end of the dress rehearsal the director had said playfully to his leading actor: 'A touch ham, Eric.' Porter, who was, not unnaturally, fairly tense, chased him out of the theatre and all the way up King Street to the Tramway Centre, still in his flowing white beard and billowing robes. I do wish that Dr Jonathan could have provoked a similar impromptu performance this time along the Waterloo Road. I would have paid good money.

Along with Liz Robertson, Michael Williams and Judi Dench, Thomas Allen, Jane Lapotaire, Stephen Fry and the Dank-worths, David Firth and I were part of an entertainment organized for Sam Wanamaker's Globe Theatre at a Middle Temple feast. Firth was once in Jonathan Miller's prized pro-duction of *Measure for Measure*. It toured and eventually reached Barrow-in-Furness in a theatre not too unlike a working-men's club. The manager-compère greeted the Good Doctor with, 'Will you need the microphone to introduce your acts, Mr Miller?'

It was a good night at the Middle Temple. According to John Manningham, the seventeenth-century lawyer, *Twelfth Night* was commissioned by lawyers there and performed in hall at a feast on 2 February 1602. Some years ago, Donald Wolfit gave a performance of the play for the Queen Mother in this same room, and there in the early 60s I spotted a baby Michael Crawford as Feste in Colin Graham's production. This occasion gave me a chance to programme an excerpt from *No Bed for Bacon* in order to hear Dame Judi speak

Viola's willow cabin speech once more. If you are looking for a recipe for goose pimples, this is it.

Manningham's diaries contain the only known contemporary anecdote about Shakespeare. I'm not saying that it is true. A woman fell for Burbage when he was playing Richard Crookback and made a date to see him (under the name of Richard III) at her house after the show. Shakespeare overheard this, got to her house before the play had ended and, in Manningham's words 'was at his game 'ere Burbage came. Then, message being brought that Richard III was at the door, Shakespeare caused return to be made that William the Conqueror was before Richard III'.

Our Middle Temple welcome was warm, especially from the staff. A porter comforted Stephen Fry, who was nervously pacing the gardens going over unfamiliar material. 'Bit jumpy, Mr Fry? Don't worry. Most of our gentlemen are like that. We've got one barrister never gets up but what he sits down.'

Sam Wanamaker's fund-raising efforts are Herculean. The Dankworths were in at the beginning fifteen years ago and once did a nine-city tour of the States with Sam, singing for contributions in the great houses of the Cabots and Lodges.

According to John, word got round that Sam was accepting no contribution of less than $500,000. They appeared in Texas and at the end three frail old ladies apologetically explained that they knew they were expected to give half a million each, but would it be all right if they gave half a million between them? Sam graciously agreed.

Arthur Smith supplied me with the first Shakespearian 'knock knock' joke I'd heard. 'Who's there?' 'Mandy.' 'Mandy who?' 'Man delights not me, nor women neither.' Could anybody improve on that from the folio, I wondered.

With the advent of summer the first alternative Shakespearian 'knock knocks' arrived: 'Who's there?' 'Howie.' 'Howie who?' 'How weary, stale, fat and unprofitable seem to me all the uses of this world.' And: 'Moron' – 'More honoured in the breach than the observance.'

We closed with too many Toby or not Tobys, too many triple Tamaras, too many Leon Macduffs: but spare a chuckle for Jane Farrell's 'Ida.' 'Ida who?' 'Ida rather be a dog and obey the moon than such a Roman.' Frank Courtney's ''Tis one.' ''Tis one what?' ''Tis one thing to be tempted, Escalus, another thing to fall.' And Robert Simmond's 'Otis.' 'Oh, 'tis foul in here.'

HAVE YOU EVER found yourself telling someone a story which they told you a few years before and getting it hopelessly wrong? At Lady Harlech's garden party for the Crusade Charity preview of *Anything Goes* I met Allan Davis, the director of *No Sex Please, We're British, Spring and Port Wine* and *A Touch of Spring*.

I launched myself into a story about J B Priestley and his pre-war play *Johnson Over Jordan* with music by William Walton and so on. Davis stopped me pre-emptorily. He was the original stage manager and my source for the story. The play was not *Johnson Over Jordan*, it was *They Came To A City*. The composer was not Walton, it was Benjamin Britten. It was the glittering production of that late-30s season. Not only was Priestley at the top of his popularity, the director was the autocratic wunderkind of his day, Basil Dean. The stars were Ralph Richardson and Edna Best. (The well-endowed Miss Best kept brushing past Davis in the wings and saying: 'I do find Ralph so attractive, don't you?')

At least I got the gist of the story right. After a triumphant first reading, Priestley left for Europe in high spirits. Dean went to work and threw in every trick he knew. Britten's score added an extra dimension of reverence. The revolutionary lighting produced a spiritual effect at the end, as Richardson's Everyman marched over into the azure empyrean.

Excitement ran high. The Great Man returned from the continent for the dress rehearsal. The over-produced little play proceeded smoothly to its shatteringly beautiful climax. As the curtain fell, Priestley turned to Dean and said: 'Well, Basil, you've buggered that!'

He was right. It didn't run – nor, as it turned out, did I. What you have just read is how I recorded Allan Davis's correction in my *Times* column (I spelt his name incorrectly too), and I repeated my original mistake.

Now for the record and particularly for Miss Googie Withers and Lady Richardson, who have been phoning poor Davis in a fury and blaming him, the unsuccessful Priestley play in question was not *They Came to a City*, it was *Johnson Over Jordan* (1939). Directed by Basil Dean, it had music by Benjamin Britten and Davis, who was the stage manager, confirms his 'very modern discordant music for the decadent second act nightclub scene'. (Worth resurrecting?)

'I well remember the slim, young (25) blond, curly haired, casually dressed composer sitting at the grand piano backstage – not at all a Basil Dean type. Dean's *galère* was aggressively normal, or so he thought.' *Johnson Over Jordan* starred Ralph Richardson, Edna Best and Victoria Hopper. Lady Richardson said: 'Ralph was never in *They Came to a City* ... That was a rotten play!' But Googie Withers was incensed because she *did* star in it, with John Clements in 1943. It ran for 278 performances and she said it was by no means a flop. Mind you, some of my correspondents agreed with Lady Richardson.

Dermott Barry, writing from Dublin, described *They Came to a City* as 'poor stuff. Priestley at his worst – verbose and idealistic.' David Kirk, a theatrical producer also mentioned another play, *Music at Night*, for which a theatrical score was written. 'That was not successful either, but I think Priestley usually blamed the war and the early days of the blackout ... For a socialist Priestley was a very hard businessman, still charging repertory companies a ten per cent royalty for *Dangerous Corner*, a play for which he said he wouldn't cross the street to see a performance, when it was thirty years old.'

No wonder Priestley could afford to make his familiar boast

when he was asked what he would do if he won £100,000. 'I've got £100,000,' he replied grumpily. 'Yes, but what if you won another £100,000?' 'I've got another £100,000.'

AT DRURY LANE we had a long rewarding day in June 1989, climaxing in perhaps the most impressive charity concert I have seen at that theatre. The first half of the programme covered ground already charted in *Side by Side by Sondheim*, but for this Artists Against Aids gala for the Milestone Hospice in Edinburgh, Astra Blair had persuaded Sondheim to release material from the four musicals he had written since 1976, of which only *Sweeney Todd* had been seen here in a professional production. Keith Warner, who staged *Pacific Overtures* at the Coliseum, pushed along a businesslike, low-key rehearsal with a company of well over a hundred (including the D'Oyly Carte Opera Chorus, the Anthony van Laast Dancers, and the London Sinfonietta). Extra drama was added as Eartha Kitt could not leave New York until Sunday morning, and no one was quite sure whether she would land in time.

Vignettes I shall treasure include Sondheim prowling the aisles, checking tempi, encouraging soloists, and giving his usual precise, constructive but firm comments; and eavesdropping on the first appreciative meeting between Sondheim (great composer) and Simon Rattle (great conductor), who was on hand to conduct the Sinfonietta for his wife, Elise Ross. There was a rewarding mix of operatic and musical performers, and the sensitivity and enthusiasm which Rattle lavished on 'Greenfinch' was a revelation. 'Conductors are getting younger,' I muttered to Sondheim. 'And *nicer*,' he said smartly.

Predictably, show stoppers included Elaine Stritch, whose agonized perfectionism in rehearsal produces an immaculate, casual performance; Maria Friedman's 'Broadway Baby', Sally Burgess's 'Madame', and Petula Clark Sending In The Clowns. The original New York and London Sweeneys, Len Cariou and Denis Quilley, preceded with hits from *Merrily*

We Roll Along. Martyn Smith sang 'Good Thing Going'. A deft satirical trio sent up the Kennedy Camelot in 'Bobby and Jackie and Jack, the first First Family with class'. Along the way Sondheim rhymed 'Leontyne Price-to-sing a medley from Meistersing-ers'.

Excerpts from *Into the Woods* revealed it to be in many ways his wisest and wittiest score so far, and Dirk Bogarde, introducing those songs, got a huge laugh simply by saying: 'Bonnie Langford *is* Red Riding Hood.'

Martyn Lewis was the other presenter to stop the show with his 'Nine O'Clock Sondheim News', written by Neil Shand. 'Good evening, in a statement today Mrs Thatcher said "I've faced Spaniards who're hairy and Gen'ral Galtieri, but I'm here/I've faced Parkinson's blind dates and my fat neighbour's bank rates, and I'm here/I've had caps on my teeth/Now I can out-grin Edward Heath/and for year after year after year/I'll stay here".'

Eartha Kitt did touch down in time, and her untampered 'I'm Still Here', rapturously received, gave me a quick flash-back to New York in 1977, when Sammy Davis Jr came back-stage at *Side by Side* in New York and said: 'Do ask Stephen if he'll rewrite the lyrics for a man. If he can't, I'll get Sammy Cahn to do it. Tell him I could make it as big as "Mr Bojangles".' Mr Sondheim passed.

The readiness of artists to support the Aids charities is heart-warming. One of the dancers invited to take part was called very early in the morning, and, blearily collecting himself, inquired anxiously: 'Do I have to have it to be in it?'

Sad, though, that few of the papers who carried stories or pictures of the event mentioned the charity.

IN ONE OF my youth improvement schemes I took Robert Elms, a regular on 'Loose Ends', to see *The Merchant of Venice* at the Phoenix Theatre. Elms, a devotee of film, has never been convinced by stage performances ('I can tell they're acting'). The Shakespearian convention, and in particular the verse, gave him a different entry point which did not challenge, indeed transcended, his film-imbibed obsession with simulated reality. He was lucky, at first go, to catch a Shylock recognizable as a screen hero but who grafted with wit and intelligence at the verse, a gracious Portia, and the best Gratiano he is ever likely to clap eyes on.

Seeing Hoffman sharpening his knives on the sole of his shoe reminded me of the handing down of effective bits of theatrical 'business'. Sir Donald Wolfit, whose original idea of Shylock was to play him as a passionate, young Sephardic Jew, untimely widowed and the one-parent father of an immature and vulnerable daughter, was a great recorder, as well as an inspired inventor, of business. I vividly remember his curiosity when I had seen Ralph Richardson's Jew in a halting production at the Haymarket. Wolfit and Richardson had an early association in the company of an old manager, Charles Doran, and disliked each other. Donald wanted to know if Richardson had dropped his knife with a clatter as he left the courtroom. 'Oh yes,' I said, 'it was a marvellous moment.' 'Ah ha!' said Wolfit, nodding in satisfaction as if he had caught a criminal in the act. 'Doran's business!'

DAME JUDI DENCH'S revival of *Look Back in Anger* at the enormous Coliseum was a triumph, with Emma Thompson unbearably moving in the last scene. People were talking of a West End run and a movie and of course it transferred and was televized. In his splendid autobiography (when *do* we get the next volume?) John Osborne has a story of Richard Burton, who played Jimmy Porter in the film. 'Someone suggested that Burton be invited to lead a National Welsh Theatre. A distinguished leader of the principality asked what were Burton's qualifications. It was explained that he had played Henry V at Stratford and a Hamlet at the Old Vic applauded by Churchill. The reply, which evoked no surprise, was: Yes, I see that, but what has he done in Wales?'

Other questions were raised too. Several correspondents

advised me that, contrary to Peter O'Toole's assertion, Richard Burton did not get a wartime Oxford rugby Blue. Colin Preece of Bury St Edmunds was up with him from April till September 1944 and, as he points out, it was 'an excellent cricket season'.

Tom Baxter-Wright checked the *Playfair Rugby Annual* for wartime Blues. No Burton, no Jenkins. However, later in 1947 Burton did deliberate: 'Should he get back into Oxford and try for a First and a rugby Blue?'

Baxter-Wright also queried my reference to a Steele-Bodger team in 1944. Before the Varsity match, Oxford usually played Major Stanley's XV. Mickey Steele-Bodger did not go to Cambridge until 1945. When he came down he decided that Cambridge needed a game like Stanley's – hence the Steele-Bodger XV. How illustrious was Burton's rugby-playing career?

Sally Burton wrote further to illuminate the whole matter of Richard's rugby.

At Oxford he spent most of his spare time 'plotting his way into the OUDS' but in the RAF '... his CO was a rugby fanatic and his prowess got him out of various scrapes and into a cushy posting – education and vocational officer, RAF Compton Bassett', where 'he did little else but play rugby'.

Bleddwyn Williams, in his autobiography, wrote: 'Had Richard's career taken a different turn he might well have played for Wales.' In this connection Brook Williams always claimed that when Bleddwyn's book was taken off the shelf, it automatically fell open at the page on which Richard was mentioned so favourably. 'Brook once put this to Richard, who hotly denied it. However, Richard went to the bookshelf, took out the book and, to his lasting delight, discovered that Brook was right.'

ONE SUMMER NIGHT I was propelled by some innate sense of symmetry, history, duty – call it what you will – to Holland House. I was also propelled by a threat from Fenella Fielding, who admired Peter Benedict, the director of the production of

Romeo and Juliet which was going on in the grounds. A massive tent covered what the Blitz had left of the old house, and temple-haunting martlets from some rival production dive-bombed cast and audience throughout the play.

In the late eighteenth century the mansion passed to the Fox family and Henry Fox was created Baron Holland. As a corrupt Paymaster General to the armed forces he made himself a great fortune. When he was injured in a pistol duel he cried out: 'Egad, Sir! It would have been all over with me had we not charged our weapons with government powder.'

I don't know what the Hollands, Foxes and Addisons would have made of Benedict's production of *Romeo*. The Montagues were variously black. Romeo was a tall, pale Indian in tight, striped, Lycra cycling shorts and metal motorbike shin-guards (possibly donated by a couple of despatch riders sitting in front of me in the audience, though they were not listed among the many trendy clothing suppliers at the back of the programme). The Capulets were generally white and the Montague masks at their ball were imaginative variations on Black and White Minstrel make-up. Ghetto-blasters were much in evidence and the prologue and the Queen Mab speech delivered to their rap accompaniment.

My final reaction lay somewhere between two of the sharper lines delivered at Lady Holland's dinner table. When a cross-eyed woman asked Talleyrand how the confusing political affairs in France were going he said: '*Comme vous voyez, madame.*' And when Dickens told her ladyship that he was going all the way to America she inquired: 'Why do you not go down to Bristol? There are plenty of third and fourth class persons there.'

Anne Treadwell as the nurse gave by far the most convincing performance; this gladdened me because getting an Equity card is an exercise fraught with challenge and humiliation for young actors, and I had last heard of Treadwell, a plump, jolly Australian girl, working her ticket by singing 'It's Raining Men' in various doubtful pub venues, surrounded by four semi-naked go-go boys who were on a similar quest. I wonder how she would have fared with Nancy Mitford's Uncle Matthew who, when he saw *Romeo*, 'cried copiously throughout,' and, 'judged the tragedy to be "all the fault of that damn padre and the silly old fool of a nurse – I bet she was an RC too – dismal old bitch!"'

I AM ANNOYED when, with every new production of *Othello* critics refer to Iago as an NCO, suggesting a corporal or, at most, a sergeant. He is described by Shakespeare as an 'ancient' from the French *ancien*, a corrupt version of ensign. In the first scene he is looking for the next step on the promotion ladder to lieutenant.

As far back as 1513 an ensign was the lowest form of commissioned officer in the infantry. By 1596, eight years before Shakespeare's play, an ancient was a significant officer, a standard-bearer, not a jumped-up corporal.

I can't see the average commander winning wars and influencing history with too close a relationship with the sergeant's mess.

Marshal of the RAF Lord Trenchard's friendship with A/C 338171 ('May I call you 338') Shaw was not at all the same thing, nor Montgomery's regard for Chief Petty Officer A P Herbert of the Thames River Police, nor Eisenhower's affair with his army driver, Kay Summersby.

Alexander the Great's lifelong relationship with the man whom he promoted from royal bodyguard to second in command, Hephaestion, seems nearer the mark.

The chairman of the US Joint Chiefs of Staff appointed in 1989, General Colin Powell, is black. I wonder how long it will be before we have an innovative *Othello* substituting Colombia for Cyprus.

KENNETH BRANAGH CAN be wonderfully wicked and funny about his fellow actors, but try to trap him into some indiscretion about his company or the three distinguished thespians whom he employed to direct Shakespeare for the first time and it is very hard to catch him out.

For anyone who has been on Mars, Branagh is the Belfast boy who shot to stardom in *Another Country*, went to the RSC, made a dim film and invested £15,000 from his fee in founding the Renaissance Theatre Company with a fellow actor, David Parfitt. Best known on television as Guy Pringle in *Fortunes of War*, he was bedevilled by the label 'the new Olivier', and didn't help to lose it by announcing his intention to film *Henry V*.

Among his latest ventures Dame Judi Dench directed *Much Ado*, Geraldine McEwan, *As You Like It* and Derek Jacobi, *Hamlet*. The idea of using celebrated actors hit the partners as they were driving up West Hill in Putney and laughing about a piece of pretentious director-speak. The three plays opened in Birmingham, attracted an enthusiastic press and packed houses across the country, barnstormed Elsinore under the proud eye of the company's patron, Prince Charles, and fetched up at the Phoenix Theatre for a ten-week season with £250,000 in advance bookings.

I asked how Branagh's distinguished employees had fared. It took time to get through a young man's protective concern for his senior protégés and reach a young man's sharp-eyed perception of their strengths and foibles.

I tried a dirty trick involving a betrayed confidence. (I was learning about journalism slowly.) A few weeks earlier Dame Judi moaned to me that she was having trouble getting her Benedick to pronounce 'whipped' properly. Branagh would say 'wipped'. Later she sent me a postcard of Sarah Bernhardt in drag and wrote on the back that it was Branagh as Benedick worrying about how to say, 'Whipped? Why, what's his offence?' Branagh laughed a good deal when I showed him the card and let his loyalty to Dame Judi slip a bit.

He was vivid about her dismay at the first preview in Birmingham. It was in the tiny studio theatre and he could see her pale, agonized face mouthing every word. (Jacobi was to do the same through *Hamlet*.) The audience hardly laughed at all and she described the evening as 'like a pile-up on the M1' and vowed that she would never direct again. The next day she gave some very perceptive notes. (Branagh's whole scheme is based on actors steeped in the Shakespearean tradition passing it on to the next generation.) The second and subsequent performances were delights and then the Dame wanted to direct everything in sight.

'She is very bossy and schoolmarmish and her highest praise is a "VGI",' for 'very good indeed'. He gave an acute impersonation of her steely glare when a note is *not* complimentary, 'The look and the laugh...' (pause: firmly) '... No! No! Don't discuss it!' Some sure instinct in good actors enables them to use that sort of shorthand to one another and know what they are talking about.

Like her two fellow directors she has been conscientious in visiting her production every few weeks. As he says, 'The car is being serviced as we drive it.' She was livid when she saw them in Brighton, took a sheaf of notes and then found the company were all speeding back to London and disinclined to hear them.

Geraldine McEwan was 'Sweet and reserved and ... *made of steel!*' She has exquisite taste, 'and takes a long time to find the exact word to describe what she wants.' Her technique when confronted by an effect she didn't like was to look cruelly wounded – Branagh conjured up a piteous expression – until the offender was shamed into doing her bidding. She was the most patient listener as actors rambled on, 'and, let's face it, most actors will talk out of their backsides given the chance'.

Derek Jacobi's involvement again underlined the company's sense of tradition. On hearing what roles Branagh was playing he said, 'Ah! my parts,' and then remembered John Gielgud saying the same to him some years before. Branagh pointed out in another neat flash of mimicry how cannily Jacobi receives an actor's suggestion. 'Lovely idea! ... Yes, try it...? I see ... No, it doesn't work!'

Summing up his end-of-term report on his director débutantes Branagh compared Judi to Tyrone Guthrie. There was an air-sea rescue on the coast of Denmark right by the open air *Much Ado* at an Elsinore matinee and she'd have liked to have kept it in.

Geraldine's parallel was Peter Brook and Derek he twinned with Olivier, 'Blocking the moves of the play with immense speed and then filling in details with a white lightning of perception.' He is always on stage demonstrating and dispensing wisdom confidentially, never in the stalls.

Branagh was already planning his next season and he had a book to write; but some of the fund-raising responsibility was taken off his shoulders by a philanthropic stock-broker, Stephen Evans, given to insider language; 'We'll need a short sixty, Ken.' 'What's a short sixty, Stephen?' 'Fifty-six grand.' Or 'We can go to bed with various people, Ken. We can go to bed with the Arts Council or we can go to bed alone.'

Talking of going to bed, I told him that there was a persuasive rumour that he always fell in love with his leading ladies. Did that pose problems now that there were three? He wasn't going to be caught in that Judgement of Paris and chuckled. 'Call it an insurance policy,' he said. Readers will know he married Emma Thompson who was not in that line-up.

I HADN'T HAD time to read his book *Beginnings* when I gleaned that he had asked the Prince of Wales how to play the young Henry V when he did it at the RSC. Later he enrolled him as patron of his Renaissance company, and asked him to attend a day's filming of *Henry – The Movie* (I see someone is calling it a remake). Although he had already shot the speech on kingship, my spies told me he staged it again for the Prince of Wales's benefit. A text on the lines 'Uneasy lies the head that does not yet wear the crown' might have been appreciated.

WE HAD A wonderful first few days of the 'Jeffrey Bernard is Peter O'Toole' play with O'Toole in tremendous form. The

reunion between interpreter and subject was touching. It happened over lunch at the Groucho. 'I want you to know, Jeff,' said O'Toole, 'that I have no intention of doing an impersonation of you.'

'Just as well,' said Bernard, 'I have been doing an impersonation of you since we met thirty odd years ago.'

There was some rivalry between the two men back in the dark ages over a little vamp who used to rhapsodize to Jeff about somebody called Peter and to Peter about somebody called Jeff. Peter could not remember her name – which was extraordinary since his command of a marathon script is awesome. Perhaps Jeff, could, although I thought it unlikely. Anyway, they used to snarl at each other across the bar of the pub next door to the Old Vic ages ago. Mr Bernard allowed

JOHN MINNION

Mr O'Toole to do a bit of research. 'Left hand cigarette, right hand vodka glass, correct, Jeff?'

'Correct.'

Later Bernard remembered the name of the lady in question. He used an interesting mnemonic. He married her. (Second Wife.) Eavesdropping Keith Waterhouse told of another man who once divorced an actress who slept around. Asked whom he was naming, the chap said simply: '*Spotlight!*'. For civilians that is the comprehensive actor's directory.

Jeffrey was showing signs of nervousness when we went to Brighton to unveil the play at the Theatre Royal. He asked Keith Waterhouse five times if he should wear a dinner jacket for the London first night. Keith had still not decided.

Peter O'Toole's main difficulty was learning to iron a shirt on stage, which prompted a bizarre memory of his early career. In the '50s he played Jimmy Porter at the Bristol Old Vic just after *Look Back in Anger* opened in London. The play shocked Bristolians. At the end of one performance O'Toole decided to shock them even more. When the curtain rose for the calls he lolled in his armchair with the Porters' lodger, Cliff, installed at the ironing board. The audience was suitably outraged and O'Toole was briefly sacked before reinstatement.

Using the opening of our play as cover I was in Brighton to solve a mystery. The journey down was not without danger. On the train three girls not a day over twelve 'mooned' at me through the compartment window; on the way to the hotel I was surrounded by thirty revellers returning in full costume from a drag ball; then at 11.30pm, in a hotel with no room service, a mysterious waiter arrived at my door bearing a small jug of milk which I had not ordered. Assuming it to be poisoned, I declined it and considered the evidence so far. For many years the Theatre Royal here was famous for a little bar known as the Single Gulp which was literally in the wings, just off the stage. Here all the greats could take a break from strutting and fretting and drown their sorrows. Michael Redington, the producer of *Jeffrey Bernard is Unwell*, once found himself sharing it with Sir Donald Wolfit. There it was that

Gilbert Harding solemnly advised Keith Waterhouse not to bring *Billy Liar* to London; and our star, Peter O'Toole, recalled an evening there with Harding and Jerry Desmonde. He was 25 and Jack Hylton, the producer of the musical in which he was playing a character part, *Oh Mein Papa!*, had just told him to take over the direction.

Mind you, O'Toole's career is littered with strange bar-fellows. He was once in an Oxford saloon with Max Miller and Louis MacNeice playing the game of inventing fictitious pub names. MacNeice won with 'The dog returns...' Of course, O'Toole did not confine his escapades to bars – hotels were also fair game. When he, Peter Finch and Laurence Harvey found out that Dino de Laurentiis was offering them all the same star part in a movie, they turned up at his Dorchester suite together and chorused: 'We don't think we're right for the part.'

To get back to Brighton, according to the historian James Harding, in the 1880s when the theatre was owned by Mrs H Nye Chart, she made an annual appearance to take a bow at the end of her Christmas pantomime. 'A large woman of handsome proportions, she always wore a low-cut dress, and always bowed very deeply.' One evening a stage hand lurched on from the Single Gulp 'when her bow was at its deepest, and impiously grasped what she so generously revealed. "Now," he shouted, staggering back into the wings, a lifetime's ambition achieved, "sack me!"'.

But the mystery of the Gulp is what happened to its panelled walls when it was destroyed and the space turned into a front-of-house bar, some fifteen years ago. These panels were painted as bricks and each brick bore the autograph of a great visiting star. All the knights, Dietrich, Ruth Draper, the lot, were removed; but where? Did they find oblivion on a skip, end up in California in the Getty museum, or are they lurking somewhere in the Lanes?

IN LATE 1989 we witnessed several *au revoirs* to Louis Benjamin, for more than a decade the moving force behind the Stoll-

Moss theatre-owning group. At Drury Lane there gathered producers who ranged from senior – Sir Peter Saunders and Harold Fielding – to young and charismatic – Cameron Mackintosh and Robert Fox; stars in all sizes, from Victor Spinetti (large) to Tommy Steele (medium) and Ronnie Corbett (small); and assorted directors (Robert Nesbitt), writers (Jeffrey Archer), agents (Bill Cotton Jr) and TV moguls (Brian Tesler), to wish him a long and happy consultancy.

One ambition – to challenge Sam Goldwyn as an apposite phrase-maker – has eluded him. Let me put the evidence on Louis's behalf. When a colleague inspected an out-of-town show booked for the Globe, Benjamin asked: 'What's it like?' 'Another black comedy.' 'Do all the actors have to be black?'

Later he enthused to Jack Tinker about his forthcoming musical, *Windy City*, 'the first big all-English musical ever'. Tinker pointed out that it was based on the American play *The Front Page*, to be directed by an American, Burt Shevelove, book and lyrics by the American Dick Vosburgh. Shown Carl Toms's first white cardboard mock-up of the set, Louis offered: 'Does it *have* to be white?' When I met him at the first night of a maladroit tribute to the great lyricist E Y Harburg, which was nearly to destroy Harburg's reputation in this country, he said: 'When I put up the money I thought it was Romberg.' Plaintive on the phone to the BBC over one of the many Royal Variety Performances which he produced, 'I'm very worried, I've booked Joe Loss.' BBC man, 'Good choice, he's seventy and he's been fifty years in the business.' Louis, counting the cost, 'I know, but he wants to bring his own band.'

IT WAS A bumpy old ride on the Royal Variety Show. Its Jerry Lewis débâcle reminded me of the famous post-war Royal show which Danny Kaye, the new darling of the Palladium, was expected to steal. In fact he limped home and it was Ted Ray who cleaned up. With immaculate timing, the encyclopaedic David Climie supplied me with a Ted Ray story from the other end of Ted's career.

When he started in the business he was known as Ned Lowe, the Gypsy Violinist. After a while he found that the patter was taking precedence in his act so he became a full-time comic and changed his name to Ted Ray. As such his first date was at that well-known oxymoron, the Gaiety, Attercliffe.

At the Monday first house, he went off to a light dusting of fingertips. Back in his dressing-room he was visited by the house manager who told him that he thought he had gone very well. Ted said you could have fooled him.

'No, no,' said the manager. 'Believe me, that act of yours is going to settle into a nice little turn. Only,' he added, 'if I was you, I'd cut out some of them big words – like "probably".'

My mention of Ted Ray's first stage name brought a scholarly correction from Eric Thornton of Liverpool. I quoted it as Ned Lowe. Mr Thornton points out that Ted's family name was Olden. He reversed it to produce 'Nedlo – gypsy violinist'.

Steve Race suggested that at another time Ted called himself Hugh Nique (shades of Nosmo King). He also remembered an occasion when Ray was addressing a daunting company of stage professionals after lunch. 'I was intrigued to see what his first line to this distinguished audience would be. He began: "You will be wondering why I sent for you...".'

DO YOU BELIEVE in ghosts? The Theatre Royal at Bath was magnificently restored in 1982 by Jeremy Fry and Carl Toms; but for all the splendours of refurbishment it is the profusion of theatre phantoms at Bath which fascinates.

Bath is not content with your average 'Grey Lady'. They have one of those, of course. Her witnesses include a touring ASM, a dog so terrified that he could never again be persuaded to walk where she had walked, and a five-year-old girl who engaged her in conversation and likened the jasmine smell to 'bath salts'.

Then there is the Phantom Doorman, another eighteenth-century figure who haunts the foyer and appears only to visiting actors.

The third, and most recent, ghost is an elderly cleaner who worked at the theatre for years. No one has seen her but she spoke sharply to a stage technician a few days after her death.

Often when staff arrive in the morning her patch is damp as if recently mopped, and bar lists are knocked over as they habitually were when she dusted them.

Moreover, her death was predicted by the theatre's most intriguing phenomenon – the Butterfly. When I was a boy the Maddox pantomimes were famous at the Theatre Royal. In 1948 the spectacular effect which Reg Maddox had arranged was a Butterfly Ballet. The girls were to be dressed as tortoiseshell butterflies and a large butterfly setpiece was constructed.

One day, as the ballet rehearsal began, a dead tortoiseshell butterfly was found on the stage. Within hours Reg Maddox died and his son, Frank, who took over, abandoned the ballet. The setpiece was put on one side, but then a live butterfly appeared and things looked up. The scenic butterfly was hoisted into the flies where it hangs today, untouched by the staff and undusted except by outside contractors.

The theatre legend is that a live appearance at pantomime time, when all good butterflies are hibernating, is a splendid omen. A dead butterfly presages death.

Leslie Crowther, playing Wishy-Washy in *Aladdin*, remembers one fluttering on to his shoulders and perching there on the opening night of the 1979/80 season. On the other hand, during the run of *Red Riding Hood*, a dead butterfly was found outside dressing-room six. Two hours later the artist who dressed there was dead.

Most strange was an incident on a cold morning in 1981. An abandoned property box was discovered. The curious crew wondered what lay beneath the long unopened lid. They prised it off and released a cloud of tortoiseshell butterflies, which vanished through the loading bay into the theatre. The only other object inside was a dusty photograph of Reg Maddox. Written on the back was *Follies 1932*; 49 years is a long hibernation.

The favoured explanation of the legend is that Reg Maddox returns to his theatre using butterflies to bless or warn. *Phantom Performances* by the theatre historian and fireman M L Cadey is between editions. The next may include a footnote.

On the first night of *Jeffrey Bernard Is Unwell* in Bath Peter O'Toole came to his speech about tortoiseshell hairbrushes. Down from the flies as if on cue fluttered a tortoiseshell butterfly. I had not warned Peter about the legend and feared he might swat it as it was beguiling the audience. Fortunately, he likes butterflies and smiled on its hoverings. I'm not claiming a ghostly visitation; but it was a damn sight more encouraging than the discovery of a dead insect.

I HAVE NEVER been to the theatre in Ireland and I was struck by the range of theatrical activity there, judging by the impressive CVs when I met Irish actors for Geraldine Aron's *Same Old Moon*.

For me as, I suspect, for many of us, Irish theatre consisted of the reputations of the Abbey and the Gate and visiting companies in O'Casey and Yeats. I knew that the Gate was the home of the eclectic range of plays staged by Micheál Macliammóir and his friend, Hilton Edwards, and that the Abbey was the rallying point for all things patriotically and natively Irish. Peter O'Toole reminded me of Macliammóir's witty phrase to sum up the policies of his theatre and of the Abbey. He used to call them Sodom and Begorrah.

O'Toole may have been disappointed in *Same Old Moon*. He has a theory that the best Irish plays are built around meals and cooking scenes with real food consumed eagerly by the actors.

He once played in an O'Casey with the late Jack McGowran and had to cook him a massive fry-up. Every night McGowran wiped his plate clean. O'Toole had ordered himself a huge pair of bushy eyebrows for his role which failed to arrive in time for the first night. When they did turn up a few days later he had grown into the part and no longer wanted them. So he flung them into the pan with the rest of the food and McGowran devoured them with zest.

WILL THERE BE any room for English plays in the theatre of the 90s? In Britain and America, Vaclav Havel is bursting out all over. How long will it be before Armenia and Lithuania are flooding Shaftesbury Avenue and the Great White Way at the expense of indigenous dramatists?

So that you know what to expect, theatre in Armenia has always flourished despite massacres, pogroms, invasions and civil wars. In the eighteenth century a religious sect called the Mekhitharists specialized in historical plays and comedies. In modern times the hit playwright was Eruand Otian (1869–1926). Perhaps the Royal Court are even now poring over his *The Dowry, Master Balthazar* or, most beckoning, *The Oriental Dentist*.

The Lithuanians are going to pose a problem for the neon specialists on Shaftesbury Avenue. The best-known modern dramatists are V. Krēvē-Mickēvičius (1882–1954) and V. Putinas-Mykolaitis (1893–1967). The author whose name would really spark a power cut is N. Peckauskaité-Satrigos Ragana (1878–1930). Fortunately he wrote short stories and novels and was probably the only short story writer whose name was often longer than his actual tales.

MICHAEL FRAYN HAPPENED upon a highly original and generous way of trying out his new plays. *Look Look*, which opened at the Aldwych (starring Stephen Fry and Robin Bailey), was a departure from a sketch he wrote for a charity gala in which Bailey appeared some time ago. However, Frayn's first venture into this method of development dates back to 1977.

On 10 September of that year, the Prince of Wales was guest of honour at a vast gala which Martin Tickner had arranged at Drury Lane. All the proceeds went to the Queen's Jubilee Appeal and the Combined Theatrical Charities Fund.

Distinguished playwrights were asked to contribute original

sketches which had to have some connection, however distant, with a royal occasion.

Frayn's far-fetched entry in the programme reads: 'A special Jubilee glimpse behind-the-scenes at the All Star Jubilee Touring Production of *Guess Who, Darling!*

'The adaptors of this typically Ooh la la French farce into English from Georges Feydeau's *Faut pas arroser les fleurs avec ça, ma petite!* say they chose it for Jubilee year because it was first performed in Paris in 1865, just three years after Queen Victoria's Silver Jubilee and exactly 112 years ago this November.'

Directed by Eric Thompson it starred Edward Fox, Polly Adams, Dinsdale Landen, Patricia Routledge and Denis Quilley. It was a huge success.

The next morning the impresario Michael Codron rang Tickner and said he had heard how funny it was. Did Tickner think it would make a play?

'Certainly not,' was Martin's reply.

Codron and Frayn disagreed. Removed from its period trappings, the sketch became the second act of Frayn's phenomenally successful farce, *Noises Off*.

Look Look, which did not receive such a warm welcome at the Aldwych, pays more homage to the less commercial Pirandello and Franoni than to Feydeau but, after a hit like *Noises Off*, who would not have been tempted to try the same route again?

ROSEMARY ASHE, THE soprano, discovered an interesting new slant on the National Theatre's plans. Diligently reading *PCR*, the actors' news-sheet, she found that it was to present a new play by Paul Godfrey, *Once in a While the Odd Thing Happens*. 'It tells the story of Benjamin Britten and his relationship with Sir Peter Grimes.'

BEFORE I LEFT New York on one of my recent visits I had lunch with the man who amuses me most on Manhattan.

He is an agent there, Robert Lantz, and he was just considering re-defining the limits of middle age as he approached his mid-seventies. Popularly believed to be Austrian, he is the son of an early Berlin film producer, one of whose claims to fame was a life-long feud with a leading critic. For years they cut each other and their wives cut each other. One day they were observed sharing a table in a restaurant. Berlin reeled in shock but the explanation was simple. The restaurant was empty and having no one else to talk to, 'rather than stay silent they had an intermission'.

I ate with Robbie at the Russian Tea Rooms where he has a regular table. Two booths away the other leading New York agent, Sam Cohn, was lunching Arthur Miller. At the table in between, which is no-man's land, someone was feeding Marvin Hamlisch. One day a new maître d'hôtel put Lantz in an identical position but on the opposite side of the room. 'Six people came up to me and complained of vertigo.'

At various times he has represented Danny Kaye, Burton and Taylor, Marlene Dietrich, Bette Davis, Joe Manckiewicz, Peter Shaffer and a multitude of others. He has just signed B D Wong, an extraordinary Chinese American actor, in *M Butterfly*, brilliantly directed with restrained elegance and invention by John Dexter. 'Now ve have to invent a career for him.' The Lantz office is very big on autobiographies. Elizabeth Taylor's was a best seller, so was Michael Jackson's (Lantz had dinner with Jackson in Los Angeles but politely declined an invitation to go upstairs after dinner 'to meet ze cobra'). Soon Shirley Temple's life emerged. 'It is a very thick book and stops when she is 19.'

I suggested that representing writers might be less taxing than looking after actors. He looked tempted to agree but held his peace. Back in the period when there seemed to be a new Pope every other week, and smoke was regularly puffing out of the Vatican chapel, the actor Frank Langella had a triumph as Dracula in New York. He called his agent one day in a rage. An actor friend had sent him a screenplay some weeks before and had phoned to ask if he liked it. He had not received it. The Lantz office had omitted to forward it. Irate, he demanded an explanation. 'What can we do, Frank?,' said Robbie. 'We have no Pope.' I pressed him to confirm the story but he smiled his Berlin Buddha smile and remained non-committal.

Some years ago he escorted Bette Davis to a Hollywood function where the guests sat at tables of eight. At the next table was the ancient Mae West with seven men. Miss Davis thought she should pay her respects. She bent over Mae West in conversation for a couple of minutes and returned to announce in a voice that carried, 'She's under ether.'

He also reminded me of a much loved Gielgud story. Sir John directed Peter Shaffer's early play, *Five Finger Exercise*, in which one character owes not a little to Shaffer's mother. Some years later in Venice, Mrs Shaffer spotted Sir John taking the sun on the Lido. She introduced herself. 'I'm Peter Shaffer's mother.' 'That may very well be true,' said Sir John and moved on. There is no reply to that, but Shaffer woke up in the middle of the night for months afterwards having dreamed that he had thought of the perfect answer. Then he would realize that he had not.

Robert Lantz claims to have said only one funny thing in his life (which is ridiculous) but the remark has gone into theatrical legend. He was lunching in Beverly Hills with two worried film producers. They were looking for a writer-director for a particularly tricky project. 'You need,' he told them, 'someone with wit and style and an original mind; indeed genius of a very special kind. Only one man can do it.' He named a talented but particularly odious person. There was a shocked silence. Finally one of them said, 'But surely you no longer represent him?' Lantz no longer did; but to them it was unthinkable that an agent would suggest a director who was not his client. 'But I'm still a fan,' he told them and added, 'It's a unique case of the fan hitting the shit.' Now it was his turn to be discreet. He would not divulge the name of the director.

Strike up the Band

The most potent influence on the modern British musical – and certainly one of the two most powerful musical impresarios in England – is Andrew Lloyd Webber. This makes Andrew eminently (and perhaps jealously) anecdotable. The world is always awaiting a new Andrew Lloyd Webber musical. The last time the redoubtable composer enlisted not one, but two lyric writers, Don Black and Charles Hart. Two stories of Lloyd Webber and the lyricists reached me.

He has long had a reputation for hiring and firing lyric writers like gardeners; but apparently at one gathering at Sydmonton (his country home) two guests who happened to be writers arrived in the driveway to find a long queue of limousines which hardly moved. 'What's this?' said the American. 'Oh, don't worry,' said the English writer, 'he's just auditioning lyricists.' The other tale followed an article in the *New York Times* which suggested that Andrew had lost his way since he stopped writing with Tim Rice. 'Oh God!' he was heard to wail, 'I'm having just the same problems as Giacomo, Wolfgang and Giuseppe!'

EMI SHIPPED A load of music hacks to Glyndebourne to launch the magnificent Simon Rattle recording of *Porgy and Bess*. The Sussex countryside could not have been more green and plashy, or George Christie more welcoming. Memories of that blazing production made it hard to credit Joan Sutherland's reported canard: 'There is a problem about Glyndebourne. They pick the weakest in the cast, bring everybody down to that level and call it ensemble.' Not unlike Beecham on Barbirolli: 'He has worked wonders with the Hallé. He has transformed it into the finest chamber orchestra in the country.'

Edward Dent also had harsh words for Glyndebourne: 'Even the pianists have swollen heads,' he said. Not the one who accompanied Willard White and Cynthia Hamon in 'Bess, you is my woman ... I loves you Porgy'. The singing was exquisite, but I hadn't bargained for the amount of emotion it unleashed in Miss Hamon. A fountain of tears deluged her cheeks as the song ended and I instantly forgave her for greeting me earlier with: 'Hallo, Humphrey.' The refreshment car attendant was no better on the journey home. 'Excuse me, sir, but my colleague thinks you were in television a very, very long time ago.' Succour came from a young taxi driver (three months' experience) on the way from Victoria to Angus McBean's exhibition of photographs at Cecil Court. 'You're my second celebrity,' he said. I asked who was the first. 'Edwina Currie.'

Angus required his private viewers to wear black and white. I have nothing in those colours apart from a dinner jacket, so I took my friend Kevin Sharkey who is black. I reckoned we made a set.

Then we went on to the Earl's Court *Carmen*, where everyone else seemed to be a politician. Lord Prior and Sir Fergus Montgomery, MP, mingled with sinister-looking operatic extras at half time; and Neil Kinnock made up his radio altercation with James Naughtie in a box. Back to Beecham and Glyndebourne. Can it be that when John Christie told Sir Thomas in 1946 that a Miss Kathleen Ferrier, who had never sung in opera, was to play Carmen, he informed him that he was 'unwilling to take part in any representation of *Carmen* which is to be made the subject of experiments with comparatively undeveloped material'? No question of that with Miss Maria Ewing.

There had been mutters of strikes among the chorus at Earl's Court all week, but none took place – unlike the fracas in New York in 1916, when Nijinsky fought with Diaghilev for a rise. The *Trib*'s headline ran: 'Nijinsky's Debut in Strikers' Role – Not a Toe will Ex-War Prisoner Twinkle till Ante is Raised'.

PS: 'Tread softly for you tread upon my jokes' is Malcolm Muggeridge's amendment of Yeats. David Humphreys was the first reader to point out that I trod heavily on one of Edward Dent's. He did not say of Glyndebourne: 'Even the pianists have swollen heads'; he said (much better): 'Even the peonies have swelled heads.' He also said of the *Idomeneo* he had heard: 'A very German sort of production in Glyndebourne Esperanto.'

BERKELEY SQUARE HAD got its act entirely together last year for the newly ordered Nightingale Ball: no gate-crashers, no mini-skirts, no bad behaviour. The square looked lovely and everything happened on time. A short, sharp cabaret with some American singers, Michael Ball and fifty violins, was topped off by Vera Lynn. Dame Vera seemed almost disappointed to be appearing promptly at midnight to sing the 'Nightingale' song. The last time she turned out they promised she would be away by 12 and she finally got on stage at 1.30am.

I never hear those words about angels dining at the Ritz without thinking of Judy Campbell who first sang them, and Eric Maschwitz, who wrote them. The tune is by an American, Manning Sherwin. Eric was head of BBC television light entertainment when I did a disastrous two-year stint there. One of his bravest acts earlier was to marry Hermione Gingold and then be devotedly unfaithful to her. In her posthumous autobiography, *How to Grow Old Disgracefully*, Gingold describes another period vignette: 'I remember rushing from the BBC, where I was doing a radio play, to His Majesty's Theatre in the Haymarket to catch the final curtain of the first night of

Eric's musical *Balalaika*. I discovered Eric standing at the back of the stalls shouting "Author! Author!" And having started it off, rushing round to take a bow.' I can't remember the last time I saw an author take a first-night curtain.

IT IS NOT every day that I leave the house with ribald ridicule ringing in my ears. Come to think of it, it is *quite* often, but not every day. However, I did pause for thought when I stepped out and a neighbour asked where I was going. 'Oh,' I said, modestly, 'I'm standing in for Cleo Laine.' He looked doubtful. 'Won't they,' he ventured, 'be awfully disappointed?'

I was not, of course, going to sing Ms Laine's repertoire but to read out for the benefit of the assembled music press the impressive music programme she and John Dankworth had lined up for the next season of their Wavendon All Music Plan.

Cleo was away in America touring in Sondheim's *Into the Woods*. John was not. But neither would be home before August and this is Wavendon's twentieth season. I got involved with it after Cleo had starred in *I Gotta Shoe*, our black *Cinderella*. By the time the run ended back in 1963 she was seven or eight months pregnant with her daughter Jacqui, certainly the most compromised Cinders ever to get to the ball.

The Dankworths' mission is to encourage music and quality. Music of all kinds. But only one quality. The best.

In the stables at their home, the Old Rectory, which abuts on the boundaries of Milton Keynes, they run concerts, readings, exhibitions and musical try-outs. Even more constructive, they hold seasonal schools in brass ensemble playing, choral work, jazz and every other branch of music that can use excellence. It is subsidized by the generosity of a vast range of international performers, a devoted band of volunteers, and latterly a great deal of business sponsorship. For example, the venerable George Chisholm earned an award for MacIntyre-Hodson, local accountants, last year. It will finance another concert by the National Youth Jazz Orchestra this summer, whose age will, I suppose, disqualify George from joining in even as a guest.

I took part in a Gershwin concert in the first season. I remembered it as the opener but Lavinia Dyer, one of the enthusiastic locals who helped to carry the first four years, showed me a record of events. The Gershwin was only 28th out of an amazing 44. John Ogdon, who gave the first piano concert twenty years ago, was to give an anniversary repeat performance almost to the day before his untimely death.

We based *Side by Side by Sondheim* on my Gershwin show formula and gave the first two out-of-town previews at The Stables. In the middle of Act II, when we thought we were going rather well, about forty people left *en bloc*. On stage we wondered what we had done. It turned out that they were old age pensioners and the bus that had come to take them home would not wait.

Wavendon is up the M1. Cameron Mackintosh, then a fledgling impresario, drove along the wrong motorway, the M4, and missed us altogether. If he *had* arrived he might never have had his first London and Broadway hit. Every other producer who saw the show out of town turned it down, except the late Peter Bridge; Cameron then backed it, sight unseen.

I HAD NOT realized musicians have drummer jokes in the way that Americans laugh at Poles, Russians at Georgians, and Brazilians at Portuguese. My new knowledge is culled from the magazine produced by the National Youth Jazz Orchestra of Great Britain. The jokes feature in a profile of Chris Dagley who, at 18, is an international drummer of outstanding talent.

What do you call someone who spends all his time hanging round with musicians? A drummer.

Two people meet. One has an IQ of 180 and admits he is a chess grand master. The other confesses shamefacedly that his IQ is only 63. 'Oh, really,' says the first. 'What sort of sticks do you use?'

A man involved in a car crash wakes in hospital. The bad news is the removal of three-quarters of his brain. The good news: he's got the drum chair of the NYJO.

Know any more, Ringo?

CAN A SONG have a biography? Here is a short life of one. A few years ago I wrote a number called 'Not Funny' with Gerard Kenny. Marian Montgomery decided to record it. One Sunday she and Richard Rodney Bennett taped a television concert for TVS at the Pizza on the Park.

On week nights Steve Ross, encyclopaedic piano entertainer, played the Pizza; but on this occasion we shared a table and I wondered if he might take our unfamiliar tune back across the Atlantic. He made notes as Marian and Richard aired other novelties. Then we arrived at 'Not Funny'. It was uncredited so I looked for a reaction.

At the first unfamiliar bars out came Steve's pencil. Things were looking good when half the television crew gathered in front of us whispering anxiously and obscuring our view. Marian pioneered, singing beautifully, while the next table dropped a bottle of wine. Unabashed, she soared into the middle eight and the battle was nearly won. You could have heard a pin drop. The song ends quietly and, in the eloquent pause before the last two bars, Steve's guest clapped enthusiastically. Had 'Not Funny' lost its chance of becoming a GI bride?

MY NEW FRIEND Vaclav Havel more or less dictated the shape of one night early in 1990. The evening started with my *old* friend Alistair Beaton demanding to be taken to the first night of a show called *Someone Like You* because we share an affection for the producer, Harold Fielding, for whom we lost a record sum on *Ziegfeld*. Harold's new show owed everything to the evergreen Petula Clark, conceiver, composer and star.

It was a bumpy night, defined by an incident during an emotional climax to Act Two. Miss Clark pointed a rifle at her faithless, bigamous husband. He said confidently: 'She won't shoot'; but a small voice in the circle pierced the moment: 'She might!'

My scheme was to get Alistair to feed me background information (wicked gossip) about another musical, *King*, which was having a rocky ride in rehearsal at the Piccadilly Theatre. He was writing additional lyrics.

The best story to reach my ears was that various lynx-eyed born-again lawyers and agents insisted on starting their many conferences with devotions, beginning, I assume: 'Nothing in this prayer constitutes a contract...'

Unfortunately, although I tried everything, Alistair's lips were loyally sealed. I took him to Orso's. I introduced him to Cameron Mackintosh and to Cameron's mother, I pointed out Angela Lansbury's back. I even ordered a second carafe – but all to no purpose.

Frustrated, I set off for the Barbican where Terry Hands was pouring for my new friend Vaclav. This was generous of me because Vaclav, according to one radio commentator, 'hates loose ends'. He looks surprisingly like his own description, 'a well-fed piglet', and the naturally intellectual son of an erstwhile millionaire. He had been to see *Singer* in the Pit and when I said I had been to the theatre everyone assumed I had seen *Singer* too. 'Was it very harrowing?' Janet Suzman enquired. Thinking of the show I had just witnessed, I was tempted to agree. Our friendship had little chance to develop because Vaclav was about thirty feet away and between us and intimacy were the Pinters, Clive James, Jeremy Irons, Arnold Wesker, Ronald Harwood, Neil Kinnock and a few hundred others. I didn't see Tom Stoppard but I wondered how Vaclav balances the Pinter and Stoppard political poles. A common interest in cricket?

However, as everyone else in theatrical London is claiming closeness, I don't see why I shouldn't. Vaclav certainly knows how to make a short and beguiling speech. He hit home on censorship: 'If you wish to see your work in performance it is a good idea to become president first.'

I got only a little nearer to my new friend Bea. Ms Arthur, the famous Golden Girl was, with her old colleague Angela Lansbury, climaxing the first *West End Cares* Aids concert at the Shaftesbury (a celebration of the life of Ray Cook, an inspired musical director). Sitting on stage during the after-noon rehearsals I had a unique rear view of Ms Lansbury and Ms Arthur triumphantly bumping and grinding their stately way through statement and reprise of 'Bosom Buddies', a song they introduced in *Mame* countless years ago. Later that night they had an equally explosive effect on a crowded house who were watching them the right way round.

By then I was waiting in the wings and remembering my first charity gala. While I was at Oxford in the very early 1950s, Greece was smitten by a mammoth earthquake. We did a concert and raised a few quid. I remember Alexander Wey-mouth behaving badly in the audience and Dame Maggie Smith, then an ASM at the Playhouse, mimicking Joan Green-wood in an excerpt from *The Importance*. The big gala was in London. We bought gallery tickets (about five shillings), and I went to a reception earlier in the Avenue Road to be thanked for my efforts by the committee.

Once there I found that I had lost my puny ticket. Lady Katherine Brandram (Princess Katherine of Greece) was the officiating Royal. 'Well, you must sit in my box,' she said kindly, and so I found myself, on my first visit to Drury Lane, perched in the royal box.

They really had midnight matinees in those days. It started well after eleven and was still going strong at four. Laurence Olivier spoke a prologue by Christopher Fry. Some colourful Brazilians danced, and I recall Christopher Hewitt doing that revue sketch about Sir Christopher Wren – something like, 'Hush, hush, if anyone calls, tell them I'm out, I'm designing St Paul's.'

Lady Katherine and party left around three. I was not going to miss a moment. Alone in the royal box at the end, I heard the national anthem strike up. I stood and basked in the spotlight which swung on to me, to the consternation of my undergraduate contemporaries in the gods, who were unaware that I was a temporary member of the Greek royal family. The music stopped. I shuffled into my coat. The orchestra played another (unfamiliar) tune. I peered over the box and saw all the Greeks at attention. Ramrod stiff, I took another call in the wheeling spots. At the end I modestly acknowledged the spatter of applause.

Since then charity galas have always been an anticlimax but 'Cook's Tour' did end with a tremendous party (only slightly spoilt when I lost my glasses) at the Imagination building in WC2. This is a triumphant allocation of space by the Bridge brothers and perhaps a great memorial to their brave and chancing father, the impresario Peter.

KEITH WATERHOUSE AND Sandy Wilson were among many who politely corrected me on the quotation from that revue number which I recalled from the Greek earthquake gala in the 1950s.

It was written by Sandy. He included it in a Watergate review, *See You Later*. It was originally meant for Walter Crisham in the second edition of Hermione Gingold's 1948 review at the Comedy, *Slings and Arrows*. 'Wally didn't like it and it was given to Wallace Eaton, who made it so sinister nobody laughed.' The sketch was about a seventeenth-century nightwatchman. The opening line was 'Twelve o'clock and everything's ghastly...' The couplet I should have quoted was:

> Hush, hush, whisper who dares
> Christopher Wren is designing some stairs.

Sandy originally wrote, 'Christopher Wren is saying his prayers', and added: 'Hermione suggested the new line, which is much funnier.' Keith Waterhouse pointed out the source of *my* confusion – E C Bentley's famous clerihew:

> Sir Christopher Wren
> Said I'm dining with some men.
> If anyone calls
> Say I'm designing St Paul's.

Sandy went on to quote another Gingold improvement for a number of his, *Medusa*. 'I wrote one couplet about Zeus seducing Medusa:

> He wooed me in every conceivable shape
> As a horse, as a bull, as a bear, as an ape.

'Hermione changed the second line to "As a horse, as a bull, as a bee, as a grape". It was also much funnier.'

THAT SANDY WILSON review number ('The Nightwatchman') started a few hares. Bernard Levin reprimanded me for omitting Beachcomber's conclusive couplet, 'Hush! Hush! Nobody cares; Christopher Robin has fallen downstairs'. Mr Brennan of Wexford thought it should be 'Tush! Tush!' They must fight it out when Bernard is next in Wexford for the opera.

Robert Bishop played in *Slings and Arrows* with Hermione Gingold and assisted her cabaret début at the Café de Paris. She performed her first number at the top of those twin stairways. She surveyed the audience and sang,

> If I were very clever
> I would stay up here for ever
> But ... hush, hush, whisper who dares
> Old Mother Gingold is coming downstairs.

The ovation then sustained her careful descent to Mr Bishop, who removed her furs.

He was also Jason to her Medea in a number called 'Sit Down a Minute, Medea'. Gingold wailed a good deal off-stage in the manner of Dame Judith Anderson and entered to fling herself at a tall pillar declaiming: 'This is my *personal* column.'

THE MUSICAL *KING* I mentioned limped to a ritual standing ovation at the Piccadilly Theatre on its opening night. A couple of years ago, in a one-night charity performance, another *King*, by Martin Smith, tore the roof off the Prince Edward. How come the Good King was banished and the Bad King reigned (albeit not for long)?

Because the composer of the Bad King, Richard Blackford, got to Queen Coretta first, in 1983. When Smith appeared she confused the two projects and gave him the go-ahead as well. Later she withdrew it when she realized her mistake and he had invested a lot of money in a recording.

I wish she could have seen his inspirational work rather than Lonnie Elder III's muddled, random, earth-bound plotting which reached the London stage. I wish she could have seen Obba Babatunde as King instead of Simon Estes, the opera singer. Mr Estes is a large, stiff, single-breasted suit with a large, stiff, single-hued voice. Mr Babatunde was all passion, intellect and conviction.

Mr Estes, or so a member of the cast told me, is a medallion man. On his favourite gold piece is the inscription 'Try God'. On the other side someone should engrave 'Try Acting'.

Mr Estes was the victim of a cruel first-night trick. Someone forged Buckingham Palace writing paper and a letter from a lady-in-waiting wishing him well and acknowledging his greatness on the Queen's behalf. You would think the envoi '... Her Majesty is a great fan of the King and has all his records, including three versions of "Blue Suede Shoes"', might have deterred him from reading it to the cast.

Still, it wasn't as cruel a trick as denying us Mr Babatunde, Bruce Hubbard, Willard White, Gregg Baker or anyone who could bring vitality, depth and acting to the role. I wish Mrs King could have seen Leilani Jones as herself. Cynthia Haymon's performance, so powerful in *Porgy*, evaporated with the spoken word. I would encourage Mrs King to listen to my friend Alistair Beaton's neat lyrics, when audible; especially his showstopper, 'They're After Your Vote'; and there would have been more compensation for her in the performances of Clarke Peters, Ray Shell and Shezwae Powell.

The nadir of this love-your-fellow-man-exercise was reached early on in production when one star clapped eyes on a fine musician, a rehearsal pianist, and said in shock: 'But he's not black!' Wisely, he left.

'We shall overcome' dwindled into 'We shall underwhelm'.

A few days after *King*'s opening night, I was reproved (on writing paper purporting to come from the Forth [sic] Sea Lord's Office HMS President, Old Admiralty Buildings, Whitehall) for suggesting that Simon Estes 'was the victim of a cruel trick' when he read out to his colleagues 'a personalized letter which, at a glance, appeared to have been sent by the Queen's lady-in-waiting'. My reproof was signed by Lieutenant Commander J J Tar (RN). Discreetly at the foot of the page was the name and address of a Jon Sexton in NW5. I don't know if Commander Tar or Mr Sexton sent the original letter but they seem to know a lot about it. Apparently, 37 members of the *King* company got similar jokey best wishes, sent in fact by one of their colleagues. 'To even the naïve the final paragraph was a clear indication that all was not what it seemed. If the unfortunate reader was not gifted with common sense, the pay-off line revealed the name of the sender in which he directed his best wishes to his colleagues.' Poor Mr Estes apparently failed to crack the code or recognize the name of one of his fellow actors.

Commander Tar knows how to sign off. He thanked me for my theatrical work which he and his wife 'have admired over the years, *The Rivals* and *The School for Scandal* remain our personal favourites'.

Special writing paper presents its pitfalls. There used to be an assistant producer on the 'Johnny Carson Show' in America whose humble job was to take calls from viewers after the late-night transmission. A high proportion came from callers who wanted to know, 'How do I get into showbusiness?' His favourite reply was: 'You have to wait until someone dies and there is a vacancy.' He used the same advice in letters, and so great was the demand that he had special stationery printed saying SHOWBUSINESS INC at the top and at the bottom, 'Everything about it is appealing'. Even more bizarre, a woman once lost a breach of promise case against an employee of Chappells, the music publishers, because his proposal to her was on company writing paper which bore the legend, 'Nothing in this letter constitutes a contract'.

NOW A SIMPLE tale, which starts in tragedy but concludes comfortably. I left Paddington for Professor Sondheim's valedictory seminar in Oxford at 2.20pm. The train broke down at Slough and we were put on another to Reading. There we changed again. I sat on my case in the corridor on Reading station for a bit. No seats on the new train. Then they could not find a driver so I transferred to a taxi. For a long time the taxi could not find Oxford and £30 later, when it did, it was raining. I directed the driver to St Catherine's College, near Folly Bridge, only to find that since I was up it has been replaced by a police station and a morgue. St Cat's is now on the other side of Oxford.

Eventually, I slunk into my chair at 5.30pm, halfway through a lively question-and-answer session featuring Sondheim, Arthur Laurents and John Weidman, who has written the book for the professor's new musical *Assassins*. This is another cheerful entertainment about eight people who have attempted to kill American presidents – a change of pace for Weidman whose previous credits include *Sesame Street* and *The National Lampoon* as well as *Pacific Overtures*. A lot of the questions were on familiar lines – sung-through musicals and dwindling audiences. Once again Sondheim declined to rise to a Lloyd Webber bait, even for a questioner who suggested Andrew has done for the musical what Donald Trump has done for aesthetics.

Over dinner at high table, it emerged that the master-classes have been a triumph. About eight new musicals are on their way to completion and extracts were performed over two days by West End casts. It might be possible to bring these excerpts to London for a Sunday marathon performance.

To recover from the excitement of the journey to Oxford, I stayed the night in Woodstock. Pope's verdict on Blenheim Palace was:

> 'Thanks, Sir,' cried I, 'Tis very fine,
> But where d'ye sleep or where d'ye dine?'

I had not been invited, so I slept soundly and lunched lavishly at the Feathers, where the enterprising chef Nick Gill concocted dense mussel soup with saffron and chives and robust pot-roast chicken with tarragon.

To work up an appetite, I strolled round Blenheim. I followed several groups of tourists, cooed along by guides. During Duke Bert's time, an Oxford don was brought out to explain Blenheim's treasures to specialist visitors from London. On one occasion he failed to show. Duke Bert said not to worry, he would do the job himself.

It was not a success. When asked about any priceless piece he muttered dismissively, 'of the period, of the period', and moved on. The guides who looked after us were much more gushing. Lowering her voice reverently, one said: 'Actually, the duke himself in person is in residence today, so if you are very, very lucky you may catch a glimpse of His Grace moving about the grounds.'

I didn't spot Duke Sunny, but it took me back about 52 years to when my brother and I visited Badminton. Our great-uncle was the local grocer, and soon after we arrived he stood us by the telephone and said solemnly: 'If you listen very carefully, you may just hear a real duke's voice for the first and last time in your life.'

He rang the big house and asked the Duke of Beaufort how many bottles of Scotch and gin he required. I did not catch the answer.

AT DINNER WITH Sondheim one evening in the summer I sought to authenticate two new stories I had collected. Madonna had just recorded his songs for Warren Beatty's new movie *Dick Tracy* and the attendant album. The session was held up because Sondheim was not happy with the tone of the piano. It had to be changed and then tuned. Headlines had been screaming that Ms Ciccone earned between $30 million and $50 million a year.

According to a studio engineer, an impatient Madonna Louise sighed, whined and drummed her fingers at the delay, and finally moaned: 'I wanna *earn* my money,' eliciting from Sondheim a bitter, 'Impossible!'

The other story is of an older vintage. At dinner after the first night of *Company* (apart from *A Funny Thing* and *Any One Can Whistle*, this was Sondheim's first Broadway show as a composer), his table lavished compliments on the brilliant score. Finally it was Leonard Bernstein's turn to testify. He found exactly the right scalpel to twist: 'Another Gilbert!' he enthused.

Sondheim would not confirm the stories, but then he did not deny them either. On the morrow, watching him at the National enthusiastically introducing Maria Friedman's brilliant platform performance of the one of the songs rejected from *Company*, 'Marry me a Little', I gave authenticity the benefit of the doubt.

Poets' Corner

The year of 1988 proved to be a bumpy ride for Peter Levi, Professor of Poetry at Oxford: there was controversy about his 'discovery' of a Shakespeare poem; some distinctly unflattering notices for his new novella, *To the Goat* (nothing ... 'can diminish our bewilderment as to what a man of Levi's standing can hope to achieve by inflicting this little book on our unsuspecting public' *Sunday Times*); and in the autumn knives were sharpened for his *Life and Times of William Shakespeare*. However, his seat belt was still firmly fastened and it would be wrong to imagine that he was licking his wounds, biting his nails or tearing his hair. Indeed, when I met him in Oxford he tucked in to some beautifully poached oysters and scallops, downed some nicely baked Cornish cod and decided, after a short debate with himself, that a very small strawberry tart would not trigger his diabetes. A scholar, a romantic, a considerable poet and a rippling gossip, he was as merry and cheerful as he had been on a very funny televized press conference defending his Shakespeare find back in April.

To the Goat is a breezy 85-page trip through a loser's life in society, in love, on drugs, in prison and out again. To the man on the *Daily Mail* it was 'a delightful novella, set in the present ... which reeks of Evelyn Waugh's romanticized Twenties.' It reminded me most of those spirited trifles Nancy Mitford sweated blood over in her early days with titles like *Pigeon Pie* and *Highland Fling*. Accused of wasting his own time and his readers', Levi retorted that 'the whole point of being a writer is to write anything you bloody choose', and in his case to earn his living by it. When he jumped over the Jesuit wall and married Cyril Connolly's widow, Deirdre, and happily inherited a ready-made family he had no alternative but to earn his living by his pen. He writes a lot of criticism and says, with a hint of academic arrogance, that he had not previously heard of either of the colleagues who savaged *To the Goat*. He was more concerned by their fulsome praise for 'my lyrical descriptions of the English countryside', which in fact were very few.

He found it odd that in the case of the Shakespeare poem people were more interested in discussing its authenticity than its quality. His perspective was a poet's not a palaeographists'. He told me a story of Rector Barber of Exeter College, a meticulous scholar and an expert on Propertius, a particularly difficult and grammatically idiosyncratic Latin poet. Barber was asked what he thought of Propertius '*as a poet?*' 'Oh!' he said. 'You mean the slush side of poetry.' (Barber was a dry stick who claimed that Exeter was 'the second oldest college in Oxford, unless you count lodging houses, in which case it is the fourth'; and whom I once heard telling an undergraduate who claimed direct descent from a medieval head of college, 'How interesting. Of course you realize that Rectors were celibate in those days?').

Levi pondered for a year or more before presenting his *New Verses by Shakespeare* and, although he conceded to me that one reason for publishing them was to draw attention to his forthcoming *Life and Times*, he was more concerned with its function as 'a lightning conductor'. When the big book came out he did not want all the critical attention to focus on an appendix introducing a few stanzas which might or might not be Shakespeare's. He still believed that they were and patiently gave me a simplified run-down on the difference between italic writing and 'secretary hand' which preceded it in the sixteenth century. The theories which were said to have unhorsed him (whether the initials at the foot of the poem attributing authorship read Sh or Sr or Shr for Shakespeare or SK for Skipwith, a minor Midland poet most of us have never heard of) were not new to him when he published. I suggested that he might have inherited a literary tease from his cousin, Caryl Brahms, who, with her co-author in *No Bed for Bacon*, had Shakespeare perpetually dithering about how to spell his own name: '. . . Shikspar, Shacspore, Shuckspob . . .'

He insisted that the Skipwith theory explored and advanced by James Knowles, a 25-year-old English lecturer at Leicester, was the fruit of Knowles's research not his and it was for Knowles to publish them, not him. He stood by his own instinct and scholarship. He had also had a critical drubbing from his old friend, A L Rowse, to whom he subsequently wrote that he felt that he had been 'slain by gentle darts of Apollo'. He added that, 'All the time I was researching Shakespeare I kept finding that Rowse was right about most things.'

I APPEALED IN *The Times* for more information on Walter Carruthers Sellar and Robert Julian Yeatman than is vouchsafed in the 1961 Penguin edition of *1066 and All That*. Most of the stories supplied have gone into my foreword to the new Folio Society edition; but B J S White revealed that Yeatman was the son of a wine merchant in Oporto. He went to Marlborough and was commissioned into the RFA early in 1915, winning the Military Cross the next year. Sellar meanwhile (born Culmaily, Sutherland in 1899) had been at prep school at Lambrook before going to Fettes, into the Army, and on to Oxford, where the two men met at Oriel. Isla Brownless, whose father was at Lambrook with Sellar, recalled one of the masters, A E Fernie: 'A real Mr Chips in the making, kindly, a superb all-round games player and coach, but above all a fine teacher of history to boys who learn at that age in black and white terms. He used to thump the desk and utter such memorable remarks as, "King John was a BAD thing!"' . . . When *1066 And All That* was published Fernie knew full well that it parodied his history lessons and he was delighted.

Sellar told Brian Walsh-Atkins that 'he used to try his jokes out on his daughter. If she laughed they were in. She was two at the time.' Bayley then forwarded a cornucopia of Sellariana, including his comment on the infant Health Service: 'Weeping and nationalizing of teeth.' He died in 1951.

His collaboration with Yeatman was carried on partly by post. Yeatman was advertising manager at Kodak when Stanley Sharpless, long-term king of *New Statesman* competitors, was a senior copy-writer there. Charles Hennessy, who knew Yeatman when he moved to Benson's, quotes a verse Yeatman wrote for the Guinness 'animal' advertising campaign:

> Insatiable carnivore:
> Oh how voraciously you roar!
> Is it because like us you feel
> You'd like a Guinness with your meal?

Another colleague, John Mellars, concurred. He 'never talked like a professional funny man. He slipped dry witticisms into a serious, often pedantic discourse. He liked to turn an argument about copy into a philological inquiry.' Yeatman died in 1968.

I WENT TO the Watermill Theatre near Newbury one summer evening to see a new musical – *Just So* by George Stiles and Anthony Drewe, inspired by Kipling's stories. A couple of years ago it was a lively winner in the Vivian Ellis competition for emerging writers. It isn't fair to comment on the production I saw, because it was obviously work in progress, but the energy of most of the young animal cast was impressive. The publication of the Honours List caused me to ponder whether Kipling would have considered a musical adaptation an honour. He had very decided views on honours. Although he was the first English writer to receive the Nobel Prize, he turned down the Poet Laureateship at least three times, and all other gongs from the KCB (which he was offered in 1898 when Lord Salisbury was PM) to the OM (from King George V in 1921). In spite of this, he was appointed a Companion of Honour in 1917 without his consent, and wrote a furious letter to the future Prime Minister, Bonar Law, ending: 'How would you like it if you woke up and found yourself made Archbishop of Canterbury?'

The source of the *Just So* stories was a long sea voyage to South Africa at the turn of the century. Kipling gathered a circle of children around him in a quiet corner and spun the tales he was later to publish. One of the best known, 'How the Elephant Got His Trunk', was the main plot of Act Two at Newbury. It was inspired by Cecil Rhodes, who invited Kipling to go up-country in 1898. It was on this trip that he actually saw 'the great, grey-green, greasy Limpopo'. Just when I was looking forward to seeing how the ingenious designer would create the effect on the tiny stage, we seemed to find ourselves in a lurid, noisy, discotheque. Very puzzling; but that is what try-outs are for.

ALTHOUGH SEAN CONNERY remains the definitive film image of Bond, Timothy Dalton looks and sounds a deal more like the man conjured up by Ian Fleming's prose. I looked forward to Charles Dance as Fleming in a new television special. I wondered how many of his friends' judgements would find their way into the screenplay?

Fleming was known unkindly during the war as the 'Chocolate Sailor', because, although he was a commander RNVR, he never went to sea. Evelyn Waugh called him 'Thunderbird' when he bought that type of car. Anne Fleming said that it was beyond his income and below his age group.

In the event we didn't see anything of Cyril Connolly's send-up, *Bond Strikes Camp*, in which M lusts after Bond in drag. When Noël Coward rented Golden Eye in Jamaica in 1948 he found it 'perfectly ghastly' and renamed it 'Golden Eye, Nose and Throat'.

One ex-Mrs Connolly, Barbara Skelton, recorded in her

diary how Fleming's appearance had altered since taking over the gossipy Atticus column in 1953: 'Ian seems to have become a very dried-up and red-veined family man. Has lost any semblance of glamour or good looks – a bottle-necked figure with a large bum.'

BRIAN BEHAN realized the importance of being outrageous. It is, of course, a family tradition.

I went to Brighton, where he lives, and took him to lunch with his brother Brendan's friend, Victor Spinetti, thinking it might help to draw him out. Putting him back in would be more like it.

He had reworked his previous memoir of his mother, *Mother of all the Behans*, as an historical novel, *Kathleen*, which had just been published. Lest the rumbustious Behan clan were insufficiently inviting he had dealt in James Joyce and Nora, Yeats and O'Casey, Maude Gonne and Lady Gregory, Sir Roger Casement and Leopold Bloom for good measure. 'I've stolen a whole city.'

His watery blue eyes wide in apparent innocence, he addressed the room on a variety of provocative issues (expletives mainly deleted).

1 'Mrs Thatcher is the ultimate in feminism. I'd marry her tomorrow if I was fucking free. Did you know she was voted the most popular woman in the South of Ireland?'
2 'The Arts Council is a wonderful thing.' (He had a grant to subsidize a play of his, *The Begrudgers*, which was to go on at Brighton in the autumn.) 'They give you £2,000 plus £20 a day expenses and if it goes over to New York I'll get $100 a day. That Palumbo will be a grand thing for the Arts Council. We can use some rich people to lead us.'
3 'I'm doing an Alan Ayckbourn. He tries his plays out in Scarborough. I'm going to do mine in Brighton.'
4 'Brighton is Dublin without priests. Brighton is tolerance

by the sea. Dublin is intolerance by the sea.'

5 'Religion is bad for you. My mother gave it up at 94. Brendan was a daytime atheist and a night-time Catholic. Couldn't bear the C of E. He said it was "Founded on the balls of Henry VIII."'

6 'My wife' (his second) 'would have come; but our day would have been ruined. She's a rampant vegetarian... I'm not in favour of the institution of marriage. We lived together for fourteen years and then she forced me.... I love her very much.... She's beaten me up more than once. Thank God she isn't here. But after being with Dr Miriam Stoppard on her TV show, I can take anything.'

7 'Women should always buy the first round. I followed three women and a large bearded fellow from the Open University into a BBC bar. They all stood around saying nothing. I said, "It is customary for the first person in the bar to pay, so get 'em in!" I never take a taxi unless a woman pays. I go everywhere by bike.'

8 'Women should be solely responsible for bringing up children.'

9 'The best romance I ever had was in a dirty, filthy fuckin' squat in the Railton Road.'

10 'I went for this job at the London College of Printing.... I lecture on modern Irish Literature.... I never thought I'd get it. I went to the interview for the expenses. "Come in, Mr Behan," they said. "You've got the job. Do you want it?" "Do I want it? Will a duck swim?" £17,000 a year and sixteen weeks' holidays. I couldn't get in quick enough.'

11 Provoking his younger brother, Dominic (who has since died), frequently paid off. 'He's sexually jealous of me. I'm married to a woman younger than him. He's the youngest and the shortest. The bugger actually believes he hates me. He says, "I do not speak to chaps like that." Where does he get "chaps" from? What's "chaps"? And he calls me a Tory Yuppie and an IRA terrorist in the same breath. He's a latter-day-Stalinist.'

12 'I joined the Brighton Anarchist Club. I proposed a meeting on "Sex and Social Repression". Four old wankers said, "Will anyone come?" We held it in a place out on the Lewes Road. The hall was blocked full. A window-cleaning operative asked a very good question about sex: "When do we get it?"'

13 'Wales?' (Spinetti's homeland) 'Where men are men and the sheep are women.'

14 'I had another play going to the Tricycle Theatre in London but it burnt down. I told them it would have been simpler to reject the play.'

15 'The hospitals of Britain could be emptied tomorrow if we used the ocean. I had cancer of the arse and I cured it by drinking Brighton sea-water and eating lettuce.'

16 'I'm on the beach every day and so is my friend, Graham. He's been on the dole since he was 15. He's now 56 and wondering if he can draw his pension in France or Spain. He's an expert on the art of surviving. He can live for a week on a two-pound tin of corned beef. He flies to Miami where he knows all the cheapest dosshouses. Did you know they have Alternative Hostels in Ireland? You can travel the length and breadth for £3 a night.'

He complains that Malcolm Muggeridge claimed that 'he made my brother famous'. The occasion was a notorious '50s Panorama interview when Brendan was drunk. 'I reckon it was Brendan made *him* famous.'

Any TV interviewer looking for a glimpse of immortality could do worse than book Brian.

He left us for a swim on the nude beach. 'The only perverts are the ones with clothes on.'

GORE VIDAL'S progress through these islands was as stately a ceremonial as those of the Virgin Queen. Scotland, the capital, a couple of television appearances and a four-poster for a country house weekend just about did it.

I had three audiences – lunch, a broadcast and John Schlesinger's cocktail party. It could be called a surfeit of Gore; but I can't have too much of a good thing.

He flew into Edinburgh for one of those book dos they hold at festival time. They put him up at a poets' retreat: 'I agreed to stay if the poets retreated before I arrived,' he said. Then he travelled south to talk about his new book, *Hollywood*, the latest of those compulsive biographies of the United States which he intertwines with his fictional families.

This time, however, a dark shadow clouded his patrician features. His sister had been researching the Gore side of the family roots. He had always assumed they stemmed from some landed, aristocratic Irish family – the Earls of Aran or at least the Gore-somethings. His sibling had blown that. The Gores were humble English stock from Nether Wallop.

All this made a mockery of his one unknowing visit some years ago to the ancestral inches. Along with Jessye Norman, Wayne Sleep and Peter Cook, he was a star of *The Sunday Times* Nether Wallop arts festival. We drove down together. He was to sign and sell his new book at the local greengrocer's. I furtively slipped in twelve remaindered copies of one of mine and out-sold the favourite son. Had they *known* he was a favourite son, he would surely have been spared that humiliation.

Genealogical studies took on a new fascination for Gore. Alerted by the Nether Wallop Connection, he developed a consuming interest in the Prime Minister's forebears. (*see End Notes*) His well-researched theory was that she was a second cousin, once or twice removed, from the late Lady Diana Cooper. Few people doubt that Lady Diana was the child of Harry Cust, nephew of the third and last Earl of Brownlow, and not a fully-fledged Manners.

Gore's theory was that Mrs T's grandmother was also within easy range of the overly romantic Harry and, since he fathered most of the children around Belton, he might well have performed this patriotic *droit de seigneur* into the bargain. The Eton master who taught Cust reckoned that he had a better prospect of being PM than his contemporaries, the Lords Roseberry and Curzon. How appropriate if his early promise was finally realized three generations later.

When the question was raised with Lady Diana Cooper she admitted it was only too likely but added privately that of course in these cases it is always important to check the precise dates. Dedicated genealogists are doing just that.

With *Hollywood* out of the way Gore began brooding on another, somewhat distracted by his rival career as a screen writer. Ted Turner's company have filmed his *Billy the Kid* (he was lobbying Channel 4 to make sure we saw it here) and TNT was planning to shoot an earlier novel *Kalki* which was for years to be a Mick Jagger vehicle. 'He is far too old now.'

Meanwhile his career as a playwright languished. Neither *The Best Man* nor *A Visitor to a Small Planet* took off in this country despite their American success. David Merrick once wanted to make *Visitor* into a musical and sent the play to Jerry Herman, the tunesmith of *Hello, Dolly* and *Mame*. He decided that it was too old-fashioned. When he confessed as much to Gore he was told smartly, 'Yes, Jerry, that's exactly why we thought of you.'

Vidal described his record as a dramatist in a neat paraphrase of Emerson, 'From failure to classic with no intervening success.'

His feud with Truman Capote survived Capote's death ('Good career move,' Gore muttered to his publisher on hearing the news). Next his scorn was directed at Capote's biographer, Gerald Clarke, whose book had been reissued in paperback. Vidal questioned Clarke's reputation for accurate and diligent research. Capote, he said, visited the White House hardly at all during the Kennedy years, though Clarke swallowed the story that he was often there. Vidal was still more savage about Capote's claims to have had an affair with Camus whom he described as 'my editor at Gallimard'. As Camus was a star author with that French publishing house, and nobody's editor, Vidal measured the value of the rest of Clarke's information against that. Gore's book, *Hollywood*, was full of fascinating side lights on American history. In what other author's work – apart, perhaps, from E L Doctorow working overtime – would you expect to find the origin of the phrases 'a schoolgirl complexion' and 'a smoke-filled room'; the inventor of 'puffed wheat'; an early appearance by Elsa Maxwell and a late one by Proust's male brothel-keeper (researched by Vidal after the Second World War); the revelation that Woodrow Wilson had 'vaudevillian comic timing'; and the news that one of Douglas Fairbanks Senior's gym buddies, a former flying ace, had three testicles?

I queried the source of this last, and was rewarded by the distinguished author with a forthright, 'he was my father'. Eugene Vidal, later an aeroplane tycoon and confidant of Amelia Earhart, had, his son avows, this strange pawnbroker's packet. It is not, I believe, inherited.

I HAD A good time eating halibut at Manzi's with Leo Rost. I
have known Mr Rost off and on for about twenty-five years.
He is a very rich writer from Florida. A liquor inheritance
provides the major share of his wealth. Tony Shaffer, Graham
Curnow and Victor Spinetti were my fellow fish-eaters.

Our host claimed to have been in on the creation of the
expression, 'the real McCoy'. Macmillan's *New Dictionary of
American Slang* defines it as: 'Any genuine and worthy person
or thing. The genuine article. (Probably from a Scottish phrase
of uncertain origin attested from the late 19th century.)' The
editor, Robert Chapman PhD, for once supplies *no* attest-
ations and many tyro-lexicographers have suggested that the
phrase stems from Kid McCoy, the famous boxer. Leo has
other ideas. He served in the 1920s as a cabin boy on the
famous rum-runners' boat, *Arethusa*. His skipper, Bill McCoy,
shipped best quality Scotch in that decade off the Eastern
shores of the United States. Hence the premier booze was
known as 'the real McCoy'.

Leo Rost also reminded Tony that his father, Jack Shaffer,
a Yorkshireman and a property owner, once asked him if he
could dissuade the Shaffer twins from this writing nonsense
and suggest that they get down to a proper job. Tony promptly
remembered bumping into Harold Pinter's dad at the first
night of *The Homecoming* and being asked by him to tell
Harold that the public obviously didn't enjoy his work and
couldn't he brighten it up?

The patriarch Shaffer was a man of great character as well
as formidable real estate skill. His tenants in one property,
Earl's Terrace, included at various times Peter Wyngarde, Sir
Donald Albery, Sir Raymond Leppard, some Russian embassy
staff, Ivan Yates, James Mossman, Anthony Sampson, Ian
McKellan and Anthony Besch. My Man in Deal was another
tenant, to whom the landlord once said, as he surveyed the
fading Victorian floral print on the stairs: 'This place needs
redecorating, but my son Tony tells me that the wallpaper is
genuine Colin Morris.' Mrs Shaffer, having enjoyed Peter's
first play, *Five Finger Exercise*, was dismayed a couple of days

later to read in the *Daily Mail* that the monster mother was based on her. Peter has learnt to talk more carefully to the press since then.

In theatrical circles, Earl's Terrace became known as Traitors' Gate. I thought the label was coined by the impresario Hugh Beaumont, when Peter Shaffer took his play *The Royal Hunt of the Sun* to the National Theatre, but when I checked with Peter he sensibly pointed out that 'Binkie' Beaumont, realizing that his firm, H M Tennent, could not mount a production on that scale, recommended it to the NT, of which he was a director.

Peter Shaffer also corrected various versions of the story which has been going the rounds for years of how he overheard Binkie's partner John Perry summarizing the extravagant plot of the play for the great man over breakfast. The book which consumed so much of the earlier chapter, 'Consuming Passions', as avocado fanciers will recall, quotes Perry's graphic account of the plot and adds: 'There was a horrified pause, and then Binkie whispered, "She's mad".' According to Shaffer the inapposite pronoun was not used, and the exchange went: 'Now they go up the Andes, dear.' 'Then what happens?' 'Now they go down, dear.' 'Fancy!'

How MUCH SHOULD a book cost? I said £2.99 for *No Train for Sam*, the master-work inspired by my childhood. Then I was offered ... *So Few* at £1,600. Mind you, the cover is goatskin, specially imported from the Middle East. Authentic, 1940-type RAF wings have been inlaid into it by a bone-crushing machine and there is a decoration of smoke trails picked out in pure gold. Inside are accounts of the Battle of Britain experiences of twenty-five surviving fighter pilots. B H 'Gandhi' Drobinski DFC, the Polish squadron leader, flew with the RAF from 1940. When he applied to be a British subject in 1948 he was told that his service did not count, and he would have to wait five more years after first filling in a form. Air Chief Marshal Sir Christopher Foxley Norris GCB,

DFO, OBE had his Hurricane shot down in flames near Ashridge. The locals thought he was a German and frog-marched him away at the point of a pitch-fork. Only when a police car turned up and the driver was told: 'Got one of the bastards here for you,' was he able to disabuse them. These biographies are illustrated by Michael Pierce's handsome silhouette paintings and Roy Assers's photographs. There are only 401 copies and you can't have that one because it is earmarked for the Queen.

... *So Few* was, of course, being produced to commemorate the fiftieth anniversary of the Battle of Britain and proceeds would go to the RAF Benevolent Fund. Those ordering it from them at 67 Portland Place needn't have worried too much about the £1,600. It included postage.

WHEN NOT BEING plied with exquisite food and fine wines or going to St Peter's Twineham church or to the Theatre Royal, Brighton, to see *Joseph and His Amazing Technicolor Dreamcoat* (still the best Rice-Lloyd Webber show in spite of a tacky, tired production lifted by a spirited Joseph from the 18-year-old understudy, Nigel Francis, on his first national tour) – when not doing all that, I was committed to reading.

I had to get through five books. I was a judge of the Whitbread 1989 Book of the Year Award – I imagine as the obligatory media bimbo on these panels.

Whitbread awards for individual classes had already been announced. We had the confusing job of deciding between the diverse merits of the individual winners: biography of the year (*Coleridge* by Richard Holmes); children's novel (*Why Weeps the Brogan?* by Hugh Scott); poetry (*Shibboleth* by Michael Donaghy); first novel (*Gerontius* by James Hamilton-Paterson); and novel (*The Chymical Wedding* by Lindsay Clarke).

Meanwhile, I also found time to dig further into Field Marshal Lord Carver's memoirs and came across an incident which struck a chord. When Carver was C-in-C Far East he received an order from Whitehall to give full co-operation to the company making *The Virgin Soldiers*, the film I produced with Leslie Gilliat.

'I happened to have read it,' he writes. 'My reply to the Ministry of Defence was short: "Have you read the book?" I got no answer.' More signals went to and fro between Singapore and Whitehall but the general, as he then was, got no answer to his question. Finally Carver signalled: 'Has ANYBODY repeat ANYBODY in the Ministry yet read the book?'

'The response,' he wrote, 'was electric. Major-General Pat Mann, the ultra-conservative director of Army Personnel Services, had at last been persuaded to read it and was horrified. Panic signals followed, telling us to do the absolute minimum.'

It is a good feeling to learn twenty years on that you were once wise before an event. Dick Lester had made a film in the 60s called *How I Won the War*. The Army, which co-operated fully without reading the script, was dismayed when an anarchic anti-war film emerged. Afraid that once bitten they would be twice shy, I had taken the precaution of lobbying Gerald Kaufman, an old 'TW3' hand, who was then Parliamentary Press Liaison Officer to the Labour Party and who realized the essential harmlessness of the subject.

He secured a smooth passage and, in particular, access to the infamous Changi barrack square in Singapore where it was essential that we should film.

As the War Officers had committed themselves to this, they could not back down even while doing 'absolute minimum'. What Carver could do was deny us soldiers as extras, so we had to recruit soldiers' sons and Singapore army personnel. If you think the fighting men look either too young or too yellow the next time you see the movie on television, that is why.

Just before Christmas I presided over a particularly happy Foyle's lunch for Sir Harry Secombe to celebrate the publication of his first volume of memoirs, *Arias and Raspberries: The Raspberry Years*. I had Harry on one side of me and Dame Wendy Hiller on the other. Dame Wendy and I had been together on so many public occasions that when I bumped into her at the Meridien Hotel, where she was attending an event at which she knew I was not due to be present, she thought she must be at the wrong hotel.

Christina Foyle shrewdly always asks a 'wild card' to her lunches. This time it was the 'stalking horse' Sir Anthony Meyer who was affable and slightly puzzled by his presence. A highlight was Spike Milligan's greetings message to Sir Harry, which I reproduce here with no permission from anyone.

'I am sorry I can't be with you on your ninetieth birthday as I have been involved in an accident with a steamroller and I am writing this from under the front wheel. As soon as they have got it off me I will be coming along as a bookmark for your new book. Warning. Don't eat the fish. Love Spike.'

CHRISTINA FOYLE'S LUNCH for Peter O'Toole was her first for someone who hadn't written a book, since that for Haile Selassie before the war. O'Toole should write a travel book, for his repertoire of stories connected with filming world-wide is spectacular. Jeffrey Bernard's speech was a more domestic affair. He was able to apologize to Miss Foyle for stealing a book from her shop in 1948. A few weeks ago Jeffrey was sleeping peacefully in the bar of the Apollo Theatre when a temporary manager checked the room to see if all was in order before the interval. 'Remove that drunk,' he commanded, pointing to Jeff. 'You can't do that,' said the lady who presides there, 'that's Jeffrey Bernard.' 'Don't tell me that,' said the martinet, 'Jeffrey Bernard is up on the (adjective) stage.'

There is a folk tale in circulation about the future of Foyle's. It might have been written by Somerset Maugham or O Henry, so neat is the twist in the tail.

As it goes, Miss Foyle and her husband were concerned for the succession of the Foyle empire. No obvious candidate presented himself until Christina spotted a young man who seemed to have all the right credentials. She got her lawyers to draw up papers and intended to tell him of his good fortune one Monday morning. Before she could do so, he sought an interview and handed in his notice. He had got another job. Somewhere in London there is a young man who does not know that he might have inherited Foyle's. I like to think his name might be Tim Waterstone.

IT WAS VERY hard to avoid Jeffrey Archer one week. On the Thursday I found him signing autographs beside me and the likes of Roy Castle and Miriam Karlin in the unlikely surroundings of the Variety Artistes' Ladies and Children's Guild Autumn Fayre in the Connaught Rooms.

An hour later we were reunited to be photographed on a park bench on the Embankment with even stranger bench-fellows, Prunella Scales and Ian McKellen. We were all doing one-night stands for the Crusaid Charity during October at the Playhouse Theatre which Archer now owns.

The next morning he sauntered into the lobby of the Savoy to host a conducted tour of Anton Edelman's kitchens and a lunch cooked by the master chef to celebrate and advertise the publication of *A Twist in the Tale*, Archer's new volume of short stories: one of them, 'A la carte', starts off in the Savoy kitchens. 'What are you doing here?' he said, suspiciously.

'I thought I might do something about it for *The Sunday Times*.'

'Another vicious attack, I suppose?'

'I shall try for something gently humorous.'

He decided to leave it to the ultimate arbiter. 'Mary will give her verdict over Sunday breakfast.'

He has a hustler's habit of prefacing many remarks with, 'This will interest you.' I was to be interested in the research he had done in the kitchens. He had watched from Edelman's stripped pine and glass office vantage-point over the steaming hobs on no less than three occasions.

I was to be interested in the meat, the veg, the fish, the pâtisserie, the sauces.

I was to be interested that he had a 'Birmingham for the Olympics 1992' tie, just like mine at home.

I was to be interested that he was going to Epping to speak for Sir John Biggs Davidson MP, who has such a huge majority that Jeffrey, with uncharacteristic modesty, denies that his visit will have much effect on the electorate.

I was to be interested that he had been with Mary to speak in Sellafield where the Tory majority is much smaller. And even more interested that he had been shown over the Sellafield plant. Had he sorted out the leaks? 'No, I left that to Mary.'

I have never been able to finish one of his novels: but I found the twists in his short stories amusing and surprising. He is better over shorter distances. This will interest you – in his athletic days he was a sprinter.

Maeve Binchy, the Irish writer, congratulated him on the success of his play, *Beyond Reasonable Doubt*, in Dublin. More meanly I brought up Hugh Leonard's comment on the revelation that Archer had written the play on a Friday. 'What I would like to know,' Leonard remarked, 'is what time on a Friday?' Jeffrey can brush that sort of thing aside with a wave of his box office returns.

I decided it was time I found something to interest *him*. Just after his libel action closed and his play opened, a producer asked me to adapt and direct a drama based on the verbatim court reports. Intrigued, I envisaged a courtroom setting with the audience voting as jury at the end. When they found, as I thought they inevitably must, in favour of the *Star*, the judge would say, 'But no. You are wrong,' and find, absurdly, for the plaintiff.

I ploughed my way through fourteen volumes of evidence, closely typed on both sides of foolscap pages. I was surprised to find that, in spite of the naïvely phrased, fragrant summing up, there could have been no question of a jury finding against Archer, unless I edited the transcripts as salaciously as did the tabloids.

'This will interest you,' he said again. Mary and he had played a game throughout the trial speculating on which lurid passage of cross-examination would find its way into the next day's papers.

'I had a call from an American lawyer just after the verdict,' he added. 'He did the same thing as you. He said he could tell after twenty-four hours that there was no way they could have found against me.'

Mary's breakfast would not, I reckoned, be ruined that week.

AT EASTER I became a judge. Not, you understand, in the style of Judge Pickles or the 'Girls-who-say-no-may-not-mean it' man. No, I was following in the footsteps of Osbert Sitwell, Compton Mackenzie, Harold Nicholson, David Cecil, J B Priestley, V S Pritchett, L P Hartley, and John Betjeman.

In other words, I was judging the four 1989 editions of *The Old Lady of Threadneedle Street*, the staff magazine of the Bank of England.

Sitwell was the first adjudicator, back in 1950. Fortunately this lavish and lively quarterly is less concerned with the Exchange Rate Mechanism and the Floating Pound than with intriguing features entitled, 'How to stretch an executive'; 'Pop and rock'; 'Gay all the Same'; 'Teaching the Queen of Spain to Charleston' and a profile of Lawrence of Arabia.

Here I was surprised that the author seems unaware of Lawrence's Bank of England near-connection. In November 1934, Montagu Norman, Governor of the Bank, conceived the idea that El Aurens would make an excellent Secretary of the Bank. Never having met Lawrence, Norman asked Francis Rodd, later Lord Rennell, to act as intermediary. Lawrence refused the offer graciously but firmly, presumably on the grounds that it was easier for a camel to pass through the eye of Threadneedle Street than for a desert mystic to chain himself to a desk.

Back in 1961, Macmillan offered the governorship of the Bank to the Earl of Cromer. His Lordship dutifully consulted a senior member of the amazing Baring banking family (which even now holds five separate peerages, including Cromer). The distinguished old gent replied tartly: 'No; after all the Bank of England is only the East End branch of the Treasury.' To his chagrin, young Cromer (he was 43 at the time) took the job.

When I finally got to deliver my adjudication on the Bank of England house magazine I was first shown round the stately parlours of the Governor and his directors – dominated by portraits of Montagu Norman, the longest serving Governor. His most endearing gesture was after the war, when Germany was destitute. He sent food parcels to his opposite number, the former President of the Reichsbank and Hitler's paymaster, Dr Hjalmah Schacht. How long before the President of the Bundesbank, Karl Otto Kohl, will be mailing much needed rations to a starving Robin Leigh Pemberton?

THERE'S ALWAYS ROOM on television for a new impressionist – Mike Yarwood, early Lenny Henry, Rory Bremner, Bobby Davro.

I am offering a new up-market one to BBC2 for one of those thirty-minute slots so popular with exponents of the genre. Mind you, my star may be hard to persuade and he will not come cheap.

I found him at a Foyle's lunch. We had been celebrating Elena Salvoni's book about her life in Soho. After lunch Keith Waterhouse and I withdrew to the Red Room at the Grosvenor House with Kingsley Amis. Two large glasses of Calvados and Amis was flowing.

Undoubtedly his best impersonation is Enoch Powell (not many impressionists do Enoch). Intonation is perfect, the impromptu script is exact and erudite, and the whole thing is spiced by a dash of impatience with the subject.

Our new star then demonstrated that once you can 'do' John Mortimer you can also do Lord Longford and Archbishop Runcie. One vocal key unlocks all three.

His only failure was Ralph Richardson, studied at secondhand. My advice to his producer is keep Amis off theatricals. There is too rich a vein of real people for him to explore.

THE PRINCE OF Wales gave away nearly £90,000 for seven literary awards in the Banqueting House in Whitehall. The evening had an ageist and sexist aspect. There were awards for poets aged under 30, novelists over 40, women journalists and romantic novelists under 35. Next year an award for first novelists over 60 is promised. Introducing Prince Charles, Philip Zeigler looked forward to something for tenth-time biographers over 70, and reckoned he'd be in with a chance.

Modestly dismissing his own best-selling children's book and best-scoring architectural tract, the Prince also put himself out of contention for the Betty Trask Award for Romantic Fiction – oddly given this year to a book whose unromantic hero is a foul-mouthed Irish tramp who dosses down outside Buckingham Palace and says rude things about the people inside.

Mr Zeigler conducted these supermarket awards admirably, sitting down discreetly when he had brought on his royal presenter and jumping up again as the television cameras started turning. No one else made speeches so no one topped the much-travelled D J Enright, who, when he received a travelling scholarship one year, asked: 'Is the Isle of Wight far enough?'

I HAD FORGOTTEN what a good listener Peter Ustinov is. It is plainly perverse to bend the ear of one of the best talkers in the world; but he is so unfailingly polite that you rattle away happily forgetting the delights you are denying yourself.

Ustinov was in London, with his hair dyed a delicate pink, to play the detective who pursues Phileas Fogg Around the World in 80 Days. That day he had been happily reunited with his old friend Robert Morley. When Mike Todd was making the big-screen version of the Jules Verne classic twenty-five or so years ago he offered Ustinov the same role. Detectives obviously have the secret of eternal youth. To spite Mike Todd, the Hollywood studio to which Ustinov was contracted refused to release him. Instead they offered him Dr Watson to Van Johnson's Holmes in something called *39 Steps to Baker Street*. 'I declined.'

We dined at the Capitol Hotel. 'I've never been here before,' he told the maître d'hôtel, 'but I've heard so much about it and sometimes, as I go past, I press my nose enviously against the window.' Menu prose which aspires to a kind of foodie poetry attracts him. He was tickled by a 'salad of french leaves' – 'Who told them they could be absent?' Many ingredients 'nestled' or were 'surrounded by' or 'accompanied by' or 'arranged with' or 'served on a mosaic of'. Best he liked 'infused'. Indeed he chose 'Pieces of young lobster served as a fricassee in a ginger infused sauce with a hint of orange', but not before he had a sturdy dish of 'Mediterranean fish soup perfumed with provençal herbs'. I am not going to tell you what I had.

After we had ordered he spotted a withered old gentleman pottering along Basil Street dressed in a very dashing, bright costume which suggested perhaps a picador or a Venetian gondolier. Neither of us could come up with an adequate explanation but it set a globe-trotting motif for Peter's conversation – a sort of Around the World in 80 Minutes. He is an instinctive internationalist and a convinced European. He was at a reception for the President of Iceland some time ago. His play *Half Way Up The Tree* had a great success in Reykjavik and he owed his invitation to the President, an actress. Mrs Thatcher said, 'We don't see you here very often,' to which he replied, 'The President of Iceland doesn't come here very often.' She then assailed him on his participation in the Moscow Writers' Conference. He presented an elaborate rebuttal. He must be about the only person to whom the Prime Minister has kept saying, 'Go on! Go on!' (except possibly Denis); but then 'The Queen entered the room and after that my lips are sealed.' He didn't know if Mrs T knew that both he and his father are mentioned in *Spycatcher*. His father has more space. He had no sympathy for her attitude to Europe. He had just finished a very successful run in his play *Beethoven's Tenth* in Berlin, playing it in repertory in German. What he liked most was the discipline of acting in a language which he knows well – but not well enough for the luxury of forgetting his lines. He found it exciting to be kept on his toes every night and not to be able to talk his inimitable way out if he dried. He also appreciated the way the German audience received a witty line which was not quite a laugh. 'There is a short, sharp, sympathetic intake of breath. I call it the wine-tasting noise.' A sort of noisy smile, I suggested. He had been asked back and intended to go.

Then we moved south to Austria and Kurt Waldheim, whom he knows well. 'People are elected for their lack of evident vices. Do the vices matter?' He quoted a line from *Half Way Up the Tree* which he liked. 'There are things that are done and things that are not done and there are ways of doing things that are not done.' He conceded that Waldheim has an unfortunate bureaucratic manner but pointed out that he was a lieutenant of 23 at the time of the crimes of which he was accused, and that Franco was a general and nothing happened to him, and 'What about Franz Josef Strauss?'

We went on to Russia via Jordan. He did a very brilliant impersonation of King Hussein. Not knowing the King I assume it is brilliant. 'He speaks so quietly you have to lip-read him?' And he remembered vividly a visit to some Bedouin in a large desert tent. The hospitality was generous but his host had a preoccupied air. 'You visit us on a bad day,' he said. 'One of our young men has eloped with a girl from another tribe and they are asking 20,000 dollars American for her virginity. We have offered 8,000 dollars American and we are awaiting their reaction.' Outside a wife sat spinning a length of tent cloth with her feet and a gleaming Mercedes waited to take the children to school.

During our Russian interlude we discussed his second novel, *Krumnagel*. (He was more than half-way through a third.)

'Publishing in Russia is very Dickensian. First they serialize it in four parts. It's rather like nineteenth-century Americans wanting to know if Little Nell was dead. If the serialization goes well they bring out a bound edition. If that sells they produce a lavishly illustrated version with beautiful pictures which, as far as I can see, have nothing to do with the story.' Here we had a diversion into book-signing sessions. 'Some years ago I was signing books at Hatchards. A friendly American in large, dark glasses and a green golfing hat pulled well down came up and asked me to sign a book. I did. "Don't you remember me, Peter?" he said. I looked up. "Remember you? I can't see you!" "It's Bing Crosby." Bing was followed by a lady. "Would you sign this for Rosalind?" I started to sign R O S. "No! No!" she stopped me. "It's R O Z A-L Y N D E – you see I'm from New Zealand." And once in Glasgow a young man took a book and flicked through the pages. Finally he flung it down in front of the author. "Would you sign it to 'The Auld Fools'," he asked. "It's for my parents."'

We moved on to China, where he has had access to many places off the tourist beat because of his work as a goodwill ambassador for UNICEF. The Chinese intrigue him. They have no complexes. The Chinese don't think they are better than other people. They *know* they are better. Where the Russians would count every Russian who did not return from abroad and complain that twenty stayed, the Chinese would smile, shake their heads and say sadly, 'Only twenty stayed?' He has a theory that China runs a much more efficient and all-embracing intelligence service through its network of inter-national waiters. He once opened a play in Billingham and ate at a Chinese restaurant there. He fantasizes about a mother sitting somewhere in the interior of China and saying proudly, 'My first son is in a very good restaurant in New York. Second son is in a very good restaurant in Paris. And third son is in Birringham.'

Our next stop was India where he had interviewed Indira Gandhi on the day that she was assassinated. He was, I think, still in the garden where interview and assassination happened. He recounted a macabre coincidence. 'Very soon afterwards I walked past a place in New York five minutes before Joe Bananas was shot there.'

One of his early experiences in America was trying out a play in Boston. He was interviewed on television by the formidable gossip writer, Louella Parsons. He imitated her beautifully too and, again, although I have never heard Ms Parsons, I am sure he is accurate. 'You must spend a lot of time on your feet in this play, Peeder?' she said abruptly at one point. 'Yes, well, I walk about quite a lot in the first act,' he replied, innocently. 'And what about the second act?' she pressed. 'Oh I do get to sit down a bit in act two,' he countered, puzzled. She pounced, 'But what about the third act?' 'I stand all through the third act.' 'There!' She swung round triumphantly to the camera and said, 'That is the problem of so many American housewives! If *you* are on your feet all day, get Preparation SE39 and soothe all your aches and pains away.'

By now we had gone most of the way around the world and it was time to refuel. His eyes lit up at the description of 'an Armagnac iced parfait, coated in caramel sauce, accompanied by a little almond cake'. I asked him if, like Louella, he did any commercials? 'Of course, and I see no reason why I shouldn't. I always use Phosphorene to finish my plays!' In Canada he made a commercial for American Express. A Canadian journalist asked him why he did it. 'To pay my American Express.'

The last stop before coming home was Washington DC. He was at the White House on the famous occasion when President Reagan welcomed the Princess of Wales as 'Princess David'. Ustinov turned to his dinner partner and whispered, 'Oh, yes, and he's off to Camp Diana for the weekend.' He then did a brilliant Reagan. I can attest to its accuracy this time. After the dinner he thanked his host and mentioned that some years before he had entertained him in London. He wondered if the President remembered? 'It was at *Les Ambas-*

sadeurs.' Some wheezing. 'Oh, yeah!... Yeah ... now, which ambassador was that?'

Apparently Ustinov unveiled his Reagan voice on the impromptu LWT show, *An Audience with Peter Ustinov.* He had a good time, 'Flying by the seat of my pants. I tried out my Reagan just winging it.' I requested a Gielgud story with coffee and got two. Ustinov was in a hotel room in St Louis, Missouri, watching the local Public Broadcasting Station. The image of Sir John swung into view. He was still touring his one-man Shakespeare show, *The Ages of Man.* He was interviewed, 'in what looked like half a ball park with a ball game going on in the other half.' He seemed very bored and the interviewer said, 'Finally, Sir Gielgud, is there anyone ... a man ... a woman ... or maybe both who was a profound influence on you. Who pointed the way.' 'Oh, yes,' said Gielgud, 'it was when I was at RADA. There was an actor called Claude Rains. He failed and went to America.' Gielgud also directed his *Half Way Up the Tree.* After the play had been running for some time in the West End Ustinov plucked up courage to tell his director that he still thought that one actress was not being aggressive enough. 'Oh dear,' said Gielgud. 'Perhaps I should have made her wear that hat after all.'

When I walked him back to his hotel he was greeted by three Americans as their oldest friend and responded accordingly. I am fairly sure that he had never met them before.

Broadcasting Counsel

Satire threatened a comeback. David Frost sent me a cutting from *The Economist*. It read: 'That will be the week that was. Do you want to create a Nineties equivalent of 'TW3'? A major independent television company is building a team of the sharpest minds around to report, ridicule and remodel the next decade. Although experience in television is not essential, proven writing ability is. Write persuasively – and in confidence – to Box 3653, The Economist Newspaper Limited, 25 St James's Street, London, SW1.' Frostie scrawled underneath it: 'Should we write?' My inclination was not to. It is a job for under thirty-year-olds.

What fascinated me was why they chose *The Economist* as the place to advertise. Is it a famous nest of satirists? When I was doing 'TW3', I once got a letter from an anxious mother who wanted her son to be 'a satirist when he grows up'; and wondered to which school she should send him. Should she have sent him to the *Economist*? Someone else pleaded in court that her son, who was in the dock on a serious charge, had been led astray when he 'got in with them satirists'! Perhaps grisly Risley or the Scrubs would be a better place to look for recruits.

I NEVER EXPECTED to tread the boards of the Windmill Theatre, but this was where Sky Television conducted its business, or at least Derek Jameson's nightly chat show. Jameson was his amiable, ebullient self, the impression that he was wearing a boxer's gum shield as convincing as ever. Two short rows of audience perched downstairs. Interviewees sat on a hi-tech set, and arrived on stage by picking their way from the art deco circle bar down a precipitous staircase. The occasion was not unattended by confusion. A lady from the Lebanon who was introduced as a Scot had great trouble in getting her deeply felt message across, in spite of heroic, sympathetic probing by her host. A pretty ex-model hostess spent most of the show looking patiently at the backs of guests who were talking to Jameson. Eddie Davenport, the young Gatecrashers Ball impresario, was keen to break into regular television. I suggested a tryst with Janet Street-Porter as a potential meeting of true minds.

I had gone on Sky to promote the Sondheim Gala, and found the exposure a strangely comforting experience. Old pros always tell you that the best television performers look straight into the lens and imagine they are talking to one person. I found this convention only too easy to observe at Sky.

I'M VERY WORRIED about the BBC. Dissension and uncertainty are rife at the very top. I had dinner with the Director General, the Managing Director Radio, and the Head of Radio 4. The source of my concern manifested itself between the warm bacon and avocado salad and the sole. Michael Checkland (DG) said he had hoped to go to China for his 1989 holiday. 'Where?' I asked innocently. 'Beijing,' he replied. I was shocked. Lowly people know that it is ITV which says Beijing. The BBC says Peking. Even Brian Redhead, who used to say Beijing, has been forced to recant and say Peking. As another more learned diner pointed out, Beijingers might as well call China Chung Kuo, or at least the Middle Kingdom. I hope this timely warning will stop the rot.

There was a goodly gaggle of Radio 4 presenters on parade at the dinner. The great Redhead himself, Libby Purves in flamingo pink, the indomitable Margaret Howard, Jenni Murray, a Dimbleby or so, Bragg who straddles the channels like a pocket colossus, and Sue Lawley who has just conferred the ultimate honour on me – I am to be on 'Desert Island Discs'.

I have never understood why I have not been asked before. (David Frost, whose ear is made of even thicker cloth than mine, has done it twice.) This is, I believe, a common form of paranoia. Herbert Morrison used to carry around a list of records, just in case he was asked; but the call never came. Every time I launched a film, book, or play, the publicist would ask which radio show I had not graced. I would say, 'Desert Island Discs'. They would say, 'Easy'; and then, as the campaign wound down, I would ask, 'What happened about "Desert Island Discs"?' 'Something seems to have gone wrong,' was the invariable reply. One day a smart girl rang and said: 'I doubt if you want to talk at the first literary luncheon ever held in Eastbourne ...' and before I could say 'no', she added, 'but Roy Plomley is also speaking.' We reckoned we had cracked it. We met Roy on the train. Journey and lunch went like a dream. I awaited the summons. A few weeks later poor Plomley died.

Broadcasters no longer live their old exciting lives. No one these days sees 'the fleet lit up' through a drunken haze. No one caught in *flagrante* gets the Reithian judgement: 'Do not dismiss him; but do not let him introduce the epilogue.' Wise words to remember a hundred years after Reith's birth.

The retreat from eccentricity has been a slow progress. It was Jack de Manio who, during the Queen's 1956 tour of Nigeria, announced a talk by the Governor called 'The Land Of The Niger'. Needless to say, he added a G. John Snagge practically invented Colemanballs when he intoned over a foggy Boat-race, 'I can't see who's ahead. It's either Oxford or Cambridge.' And during the lying-in-state of Pope Paul, one particularly close BBC close-up of the coffin was suddenly, albeit briefly, captioned 'Live from Rome'. My favourite gaffe occurred in a wartime broadcast by King Haakon of Norway to his subjugated people. The producer asked for a disc of a fanfare to introduce HM the King. The monarch came before his people preceded by cries of: 'Roll up! Roll up! See the bearded lady!' The disc delivered was of a funfair.

WE MOURN THE death of two great comic talents: Laurence Olivier and Tommy Trinder. Olivier was an expert in mining for an unexpected laugh in a tragic context – who having heard him will forget what he did for the Anthropophagi in *Othello*? Trinder was the wittiest taxi driver who never steered a cab; the epitome of the lightning cockney getting the last word. His put-down to Orson Welles during his cabaret act at the Café de Paris is justly famous. He used to roam the floor handing out cards and saying 'Trinder's the name!' A drunken Welles snarled back: 'Why don't ya change it?'

'Is that an insult, Mr Welles?' asked Trinder. 'Or a proposal of marriage?' I remember an edition of 'Beat the Clock' which he was hosting in the course of 'Sunday Night at the London Palladium'. An appallingly bad-tempered woman was a contestant and, as she grew ruder, Trinder struggled not to insult her. Bending over backwards to appear gracious, he let her into the final round, which she won. The big prize was wheeled on. It was a hairdryer. The contestant looked at it, unimpressed, 'I've got one already,' she said, sourly. Trinder's will to be pleasant snapped. 'Never mind, madam,' he hissed. 'One day you may have a two-headed baby.'

I HAD HOPED to blow a generous blast of bracing north-eastern air through these pages. Months ago I was invited by Zenith Productions to chair the pilot programme of its political quiz, 'No 10,' to be recorded in Newcastle for BBC2.

Excited by the unfamiliar terrain, I questioned nice Mr Gardhouse of Loose Ends. He, a Geordie, told me to look out for such local delicacies as singing hinnies – scones with a heavy fat content – and stotty cakes – large loaves of flat bread. Most of all, I set my heart on a stopover with the McCoys at the Tontine, Staddlebridge. Chefs and food guides rave about the wonders wrought by the brothers McCoy. Jonathan Meades, Marco Pierre White, even Janet Street-Porter, bear testimony. A recent César Award called the place 'utterly acceptable and mildly eccentric', which was enough to hook me.

At the beginning of the week of the recording it occurred to me that although I had been keeping the date free of other engagements I had not heard from the Messrs (or Mesdames) Zenith since they issued their invitation. I called one 'Andrea', the only name beside the telephone number in my diary. No Andrea. However, an embarrassed Messr Zenith explained that Alan Yentob, the thrusting young Irving Thalberg of BBC2, had changed Zenith's mind and appointed the excellent Simon Hoggart in my place. He was sorry they had forgotten to tell me. It hasn't turned up on my home screen yet.

ODD THINGS HAPPEN on Scottish television in the wee small hours – I was in Edinburgh for the Festival and I can swear to it. Irish and Australian football are popular. Both games are hybrids of soccer and rugby. Then there are excursions into the Gaelic and a plethora of ads for the Royal Bank of Scotland; and on one early morning I watched what seemed like hours of Phil Donahue conducting a seminar on plastic surgery.

In Hollywood plastic surgery was certainly up and going in silent-film days. The famous Westmore family, who were make-up artists, also practised the craft. After Harold Lloyd lost a thumb and index finger on his right hand from a faulty explosive prop he usually wore gloves; but for one close-up George Westmore created prosthetic fingers from textured latex. It would be ungallant to list those stars who have been 'helped'; but there were some for whom the word is hindered.

Gary Cooper and Mary Pickford had notoriously bad face-lifts and when Merle Oberon made *Interval* at the age of 62, critics reviewed her operation rather than the movie.

Less disastrously, Paramount filled Kirk Douglas's famous

dimple with putty in his early days, and even Shirley Temple had her face pulled back with surgical tape under her false corkscrew curls.

Gore Vidal knew the victim of one of the worst lifts. The early screen idol Richard Barthelmess had the bags beneath his eyes cut away leaving his lower lids sagging so horribly and watering so fluidly that he never acted again. Fortunately he had saved his money and married well.

The happiest story is that of Jack Palance. His very ordinary face was smashed in a plane crash. As a result he acquired the replacement which has served him in such good stead as a villain.

MOST OF MY wireless work is for Radio 4. An excursion into Light Entertainment took me back. I saw David Climie, a witty man who recalled his late colleague, George Wadmore, a comedy writer in the golden days of radio, mostly on 'Ray's a Laugh' and 'Educating Archie'. A natural wit with very little formal education, Wadmore once observed of another craftsman, Peter Myers, who had Technicolor teeth, that 'he only needed a white one for the snooker set'.

Climie was working with Wadmore in 1960. In those days a favourite rendezvous for extra-marital dalliance was the Regent Palace Hotel. Climie introduced Wadmore to the venue. One evening, after a party in London, Climie and his wife missed their last train. They decided to spend the night in the aforesaid Regent Palace. Next day Wadmore was shocked to hear where he had passed the night. 'You took your *wife* to the Regent Palace?' he exploded. 'My God! Did they charge you corkage?'

TWO PERSONAL OBITUARIES: when Ken Tynan died, his passing was diminished for those who did not know him by headlines which read, 'TV four-letter word man dies'. Mary McCarthy's obits could have been headed 'Woman who provoked TV four-letter word outrage dies'. She and Ken, never having met, had waged a long literary war. When I engaged them to debate on 'BBC3', a successor to 'TW3', I had second thoughts. Print antagonists often find they have no quarrel when they meet.

We lunched at the Café Royal and they found themselves in total agreement. Only on censorship could they rake up a difference. Mary favoured a little in the right place at the right time. Ken was uncompromising. My most vivid image of Mary is on a 'Monitor' programme when Huw Wheldon asked her about Hemingway's ideas. 'Oh,' she said, 'I don't think Hemingway was ever raped by an idea.'

I also mourn Henry Hall, who died in Eastbourne at 91. A band leader and radio personality, he was, some obituarists would have it, the first talk-show host. With the phrase, 'This *is* Henry Hall and tonight is my guest night,' he introduced acts and engaged in some not very relaxed conversation. Around 1960, as a fledgeling light entertainment producer, I was responsible for a disastrous television show which finished his screen career. A shrewd but gentle man, he never reproached me.

I HAVE TO take issue with dear old Robin Day who managed several inaccuracies in a single paragraph on Libby Purves's Radio 4 programme *Midweek*.

I haven't read his autobiography, but doubtless it compounds them. He dismissed the 'so-called satire boom' of the 60s as lasting only eighteen months. In fact there were three and a half seasons over four years, and three television series yielded about 145 shows. He selected the description of Alec Douglas Home as 'a cretin' on 'TW3' as the nadir. In fact, the remark was made by Bernard Levin on 'Not So Much A Programme, More A Way of Life'.

If Sir Robin casts aside his own autobiography for a moment and opens mine at page 107, he will find an accurate description of the event.

'Levin dropped the word "cretin" into his assessment of

Douglas Home. It became a famous red herring. Patrick Campbell first picked up the word and belaboured Levin with it. Ian Macleod took him up on the more serious side of his argument. Campbell persisted in making Levin look foolish and David Frost drew from him first a modification, then a withdrawal and then an apology.

'Frost controlled the incident impeccably and it was irritating to find an habitually responsible critic like Peter Black accepting a commission to condemn in print an incident which he admitted not having seen and of which plainly he had heard an inaccurate report.'

It sounds as if Robin suffered the same disadvantage.

Actually, in restrospect, that part of the show more nearly resembled a properly ordered edition of Question Time than what passed for satire.

The better Frost jibe on 'TW3' attended the election battle between Sir Alec and Harold Wilson, which elicited Frost's description of the democratic process as 'Dull Alec versus Smart Alec'.

IT SEEMED EXTRAORDINARY when Cliff Michelmore reached three score years and ten. He dominated the early evening airwaves for ten years during the 50s and 60s, but any viewer under twenty-five will only know him as the pleasant cove who travels a lot. He certainly kept on the move as he approached seventy, having covered Britain and made nearly fifty public appearances in not many more days and returned with pungent views about British hotels and railways.

Paul Fox hosted a birthday lunch for him and survivors of the old 'Tonight' programme and others. Sir Geoffrey Johnson-Smith was there straight from casting his Tory leadership vote. (No prizes for guessing for whom he cast it.) Sir Antony Jay was there, straight from selling his company for £15 million and probably from writing a gracious victory speech for the Prime Minister. It was Nigel Lawson who first recruited Jay to liven up his public prose and Mrs Thatcher who then nabbed him.

Michelmore spotted the Jay wit, which was to flower into
'Yes, Minister', when he was a producer of the old 'Highlight'
programme which preceded 'Tonight'. Cliff was due to interview a politician when Derek Ibbotson ran a four-minute mile
around the corner at White City. Ibbotson was rushed across
to join the programme and Jay, seeing a third microphone
being placed on the table, remarked, 'one more and we'd have
a Formica table'. Well, it beats 'the lady's not for turning', if
not 'keep taking the pills'.

Alan Whicker was there between visits to Hong Kong and
so was the last director-general of the BBC, Alasdair Milne. I
caught them complacently agreeing that neither had changed
much in thirty years – though, they were saying, I had not
weathered nearly as well. Anthony Smith, president of Mag-
dalen, was there; when he joined 'Tonight' he was known as
Red Tony, but whisper it not in the quad. Peter Dimmock,
Bill Cotton Junior and Peter Black, the veteran television
critic, along with Tom Savage and John Carter, Cliff's travel
colleagues, made up the table.

We remembered Cliff's unflappability and his ability to
conduct one-sided Pinteresque conversations on the studio
telephone when the director, usually me, had rung down to
tell him there was a cock-up and then become so enmeshed in
trying to put it right that the presenter was left to while away
a minute or two talking to no one.

We recalled the evening when the lift carrying Cliff up to
the studio jammed a few feet short of the floor, leaving only his
head and shoulders visible. Undaunted, he ordered a camera to
be trundled out to the lift so that he could introduce the
programme through the gates. Then there was the electricians'
strike, when we moved across to the open air on the roof of
television centre. Marcel Marceau's toupée was nearly blown
away, and you could see blue sky between scalp and rug before
he clutched it back on.

One useful ploy for nervous interviewees emerged. When
Cliff was quizzing the late Krishna Menon, he ran up against
the ultimate conversation-stopper: 'That question is not cast

in the mould of my thinking,' said the great man several times. Someone should try it on Wogan.

THE ROADS TO Southampton are littered with the bones of comedians who failed to make an English version of that macabre American anti-talent television programme, 'The Gong Show', work for TVS. Will the M2 to Gillingham prove a similar burial ground?

Network One and Cecil Korer (the man who brought Paul Hogan to Channel 4) highlighted two programmes which bear a family likeness. One is called 'The Flip Show', the other 'Pull the Plug'. They closely resemble each other except that in the latter the 'celebrity' judges and the presenter are encouraged to be even ruder about the competing acts.

In the studio we were confronted by: a more than mature lady doing a frantic tap-dance; General Global, who sang 'Brother, Can You Spare a Dime?', strutting his stuff in fishnets, high heels and an American general's uniform top; Christopher Robb, who sang 'Glow Little Glow Worm Glow' in pink drag, half-construction worker, half-ballerina; the Totally Naff Tarts, who rendered Rossini's Cat Duet until blown out; the Rocking Gorbachev, a look-alike who used to be an Elvis Presley impersonator when he was younger and had hair; a man from Southall who wheezed out a Harry Lauder medley; Benji Ming, a comedy musical glasses act; Ruth Olley, a female Ronnie Ronalde; Junk and Disorderly, a mad professor routine, and Potato Head, an act of whom I can remember very little.

The two winners were Paul Connor and Helen Rhodes, a quaint couple from Manchester who impersonated ballpoint pens, and Franklyn Jamieson, a rather good roller-skating dancer. The whole thing was a strange experience and was promised as a spearhead of BSB's upmarket assault on our airwaves.

LUNCHING AT THE *Spectator* with Peter O'Toole, Michael

Redington and Jeffrey Bernard, Keith Waterhouse, in a moment of uncharacteristic madness, bet me that the old 'Brains
Trust' had a studio audience. Have you ever heard of taking
sweets from a baby? His principal evidence was a Richmal
Crompton (*William*) story. Imagine my surprise when Dominic Lawson, the next editor of the mag, joined in the bet
for another £5. He can't have been born when 'The Brains
Trust' ceased upon the midnight. A quick call to My Man in
Deal produced chapter and verse.

According to Julian Huxley's memoirs, 'The Brains Trust'
started 'in 1939 at the BBC's old place in Savoy Hill, with
Professor Joad and Commander Campbell as guinea-pigs'.
For the first year the programme was called 'Any Questions?'

The revelation is that Campbell was not a Commander and
Joad was not a Professor. Campbell ('When I was in Patagonia
...') was a ship's purser. The BBC granted him the title of
Commander, much to the annoyance of the Admiralty. Joad
('It depends what you mean by ...') was merely head of
the department of philosophy at Birkbeck College, with no
professorial chair.

On 2 April 1942, Captain Evelyn Waugh, Royal Marines, a
guest on 'The Brains Trust', found Campbell 'vulgar, insincere,
conceited', and Joad 'goat-like, libidinous, garrulous'. Bob
Boothby, in *Recollections of a Rebel* records that Joad, who
was later to be arrested and fined for dodging train fares, told
him that 'his favourite pastime was travelling on railway trains
without a ticket'.

We had a better train story at the same lunch in Doughty
Street. Alfred, Lord Tennyson, on his first railway journey,
was bowled over by the talent of the driver.

'Such a good steerer, we had. We approached a tunnel and
I was terrified; but so great was his skill that he drove the
engine straight at the centre of the aperture. He touched neither
one side of it nor the other before we emerged.'

I HAVE IN my time been understudied by Hermione Gingold

and played (as narrator of *Side by Side by Sondheim*) by artists as varied as Peggy Lee, Dorothy Lamour, Russell Harty, Michael Aspel, Sheridan Morley and two glove puppets called Kukla and Ollie. But I had to wait a long time to be a stand-in myself – for Frank Warren, the gunned-down boxing promoter.

I had never met Mr Warren although I did once shake hands with Terry Marsh, the fighter accused of trying to arrange his death, a few years ago when he was made a Man of the Year.

I owed my new role to BBC Northern Ireland who had booked Mr Warren (suddenly indisposed) to appear on 'The Show', an ambitious late Saturday night entertainment which is transmitted from its Balmoral studio in Belfast. Two comperes and a host of actors conducted seventy-five minutes of satirical sketches, songs, interviews, badinage and general jollity.

It was my first visit to Ulster. My man in Deal had warned me that he was once lifted off the floor of a pub in Earls Court by the late Patrick Magee for using the word and not put down until he corrected it to 'the six counties', so I travelled cautiously. The journey from the airport skirted the top of the Falls Road but my visit was cocooned in car, hotel and studio.

What did surprise me was the range of subjects covered in the sketches and the number of public figures mocked by the actors and impersonators. Ian Paisley, Gerry Fitt, Barry McGuigan, John Cole, Sir John Herman, Peter Brooke and Gerry Adams were all treated with scant respect, and the impersonation of Adams was wittily done as a soundless mime to accommodate current broadcasting restrictions.

My fellow guest was the film critic Alexander Walker. Over dinner he told me that in 1987 he judged an Ulster film festival. He spoke lyrically of *The Best Man*, the winning entry, produced by a Catholic priest. It has been shown on RTE but not on British screens, big or small. He enthusiasm made me think we are missing a gem.

APPEARING ON A late-night chat show 'It's Nearly Saturday', I enjoyed a reunion with Liz Robertson – just back from touring America with Nureyev in *The King and I*.

She returned with immense affection for the Russian and a gross of stories. On one occasion, in a cold, full theatre, the King of Siam arrived on stage with a poncho round his bare shoulders, clogs on his bare feet, muttering: 'Now I am warm,' and turned the 'Shall We Dance' polka into a clog dance.

In Miami, they were playing the end of Act I when Rudolf barely made the stage in time for his entrance and was immediately distracted. Mrs Anna is subtly advising the king on how to convince the British he is not a barbarian. To each of her suggestions he replies that that is exactly what he had intended. To Mrs Anna's and the audience's confusion, the king's lines were peppered with frantic calls of, 'Matt – the phone!' to the stage manager in the wings, accompanied by bizarre mimings.

Liz could see Matt giving Nureyev repeated thumbs down. No way was he going to bring a telephone on for Rudolf to conduct a twentieth-century conversation in nineteenth-century Siam. Eventually the curtains fell and Nureyev sped to his dressing-room. It transpired that in his dash to the stage he had interrupted a long-distance call to Paris and left the receiver off. He was paying for the call.

The first 'It's Nearly Saturday' went smoothly, but my other television experience was not so good. If anyone had a grudge against me, revenge was at hand if they watched Emma Freud presiding over 'Plunder', a series in which people ransacked television archives.

In 1976, a BBC director rang to say he was doing a play about Michael Arlen (played by Alan Badel). There was a two-minute scene in it, a reunion with Noël Coward. 'We thought it would be good to have you play Coward,' he said, 'rather than a proper actor.' I had an afternoon to spare, mastered a few of the master's chestnuts ('looking like a heavily doped Chinese illusionist'), presented myself at the television centre, recorded it and left for America. It went out while I was there so I hadn't seen it before.

It was the worst piece of acting ever recorded on videotape.

My banana fingers flagged their presence at the lens in extravagant parody of Coward's well-known gesture. The voice was strangled, the appearance gross. Nicholas Craig is threatening to revive it. You have been warned.

However, there were redeeming features in the programme, especially an ironic excerpt from an interview with Norman St John-Stevas, as he then was. He responded to the question: 'Did you find it easy nudging a self-willed woman down the right path?' with: 'I've got a little will of my own.' An inquiry about who learnt more quickly, when he and Mrs Thatcher took French lessons in Camden at the Ministry of Education, elicited the response: 'I don't know, we took them at opposite ends of the corridor. But the Prime Minister is a very fast mover.' She is. Four days later he was out of a job.

HERE'S A GOOD game, invented as far as I know on the spur of the moment by Sandy Toksvig who'd rashly agreed to appear one Saturday on 'Loose Ends'.

There is a correct grammatical term for it, but I didn't know it, so I called it mismatches. I think it started because Ms Toksvig objected to being called a sex-kitten and didn't think the two words went logically together.

Five minutes in the George after the show provided a fair crop of mismatches. How about BBC Enterprises, Belgian Celebrity, Poor Andrew Lloyd Webber and Military Intelligence?

The engaging Emo Phillips suggested Coleslaw and Radiator, which is surreal but not quite in the spirit of the game.

Later Ms Toksvig had to justify her final contribution – Channel Television. Apparently she actually appeared on Channel Television some time back and had found a cameraman who was in a state of high excitement. 'We're breaking into drama next year,' he boasted. She was sympathetic: 'Are you thrilled?' 'Well, not really. The other cameraman's doing it.'

I was subsequently reproved by R O Harris for not knowing a better word for mismatches is oxymoron. In truth I was too idle to check it. He cited the bursar of a public school in Dorset who swore that a sign saying 'Beware oxymorons abound here' was more effective in keeping out village lads than the usual 'Trespassers will be prosecuted'. And John Koski listed his good ones from the *Mail on Sunday*. I like operator service, British Rail catering, Labour Party leadership, British tennis hopeful and working lunch.

Francis Wheen's biography of Tom Driberg threw up three new amusing oxymorons. Tom went to Lancing, said to be a 'liberal' public school. Mr Wheen comments: 'One might well speak of a comfortable prison or a palatable Liebfraumilch.'

APPEARING ON BSB before David Frost had officially declared it open was a bit like calling oneself Sir Ned before the Queen has got her sword out. However, 'Up Your News', a nightly fifteen minutes of topical 'satire' was an adequate excuse for *lèse-majesté*. An army of writers worked through the day on a script. Three actors pre-recorded most of the sketches, and at 9pm the visiting presenter read an autocue live in a studio situated roughly where the old dance floor of the Trocadero once stood.

Ken Livingstone had done the chore the night before, but the Noel Gay office walls are papered with rejection letters from other politicians. Lord Jenkins of Hillhead 'doubted his ability to perform the role'. Edwina Currie, 'having resisted Sky TV', said she would resist BSB as well. Baroness Falkender was 'no good at TV'. Busy, too busy or 'hopelessly busy' were Denis Healey, Chris Patten, Michael Foot, Edward Heath, David Owen, John Smith, Nigel Lawson, Michael Heseltine, Diane Abbott and Willy Whitelaw. Norman Tebbit was brief and sour. 'Thank you. I do not believe you will be on the air and in any event I do not wish to appear on it.'

I GOT INSIDE news from the world of American sit-commery

from Andrew Nickolds' scriptwriter chums Brian and Mert. Do you know what a 'Hey, May!' is?

It is a phrase used in the United States to describe the cliff-hanging end of the first half of a thirty-minute sit-com. The theory is that the American couch-potato husband sits in front of his set with his six-pack and, if intrigued, yells to the little woman in the kitchen, 'Hey, May! You've gotta see this!' No 'Hey, May!' means no audience for Act Two.

IN THE THEATRE for the stage version of *Beecham*, Timothy West waved his baton to a recorded orchestra, but on the recording for Yorkshire TV he had to carry the 64-strong Hallé with him. Only Jean Ball, the Hallé's harpist, had played under Sir Thomas, just before he died in 1961. She recalled a morning when, delayed by a fault on the railway line, he treated the orchestra to an hour-long diatribe on the evils of the railways of Britain before he would raise his baton to rehearse.

The day before the screening EMI launched a bumper issue of Beecham recordings on CD and Shirley, Lady Beecham, announced she was applying to remove Sir Thomas's remains from Brookwood cemetery near Woking where, in 'land-scaping' the 450-acre Victorian burial ground, bulldozers have produced a wasteland. If Sir Thomas's body has to be moved, surely Westminster Abbey should be his final resting place?

Powers That Be

D id you know why Richard Nixon served soup only once at a White House banquet? Dwell on the question for a moment while I organize a diversion.

George Nathaniel Curzon, thunderously requoted by Randolph Churchill (not quite such a superior person), used to say: 'No gentleman drinks soup at luncheon.' I don't know where he got the idea. I have lost my Emily Post. I can't believe that many people accept it today. Although making no claims of being a gentleman, I do like a bowl of soup and a crust of bread at lunch. Especially if it is the juice left over from yesterday's tripe. I enjoy tripe so much I am beginning to think it is unhealthy, but no one has yet lumped it with eggs, chicken, soft French cheese or the other new poisons, so if it should be, don't tell me.

Anyway, to get back to Nixon and his soup ban. He stopped it because at his very first presidential 'do' he spilt vichyssoise down his new tie. He ordered his Chief of Protocol never to put soup on the menu again. I suppose soup is back with Bush.

P J O'Rourke has a great variation on the old definition of boredom. Instead of 'as exciting as watching grass grow', or 'as watching paint dry', he now says: 'as exciting as watching George Bush prepare for bed'.

Nixon's daughters, Tricia and Julie, sound less boring than their de-souped Dad. A man I know once sat between them at a White House dinner, and Barry Goldwater Junior, who was keen to date Tricia, was sitting on the other side of Julie. His opening gambit was not a success. 'Have you ever been to

California?' he enquired. 'Yes,' she said. 'I was born and raised there.'

My Deep Larynx for these epoch-making gobbets of White House information was kicking himself because he left the ubiquitous Pamella Bordes out of his book, *By Hook Or By Crook*, a riot of skulduggery documenting the machinations of the Al Fayeds, Adnan Kashoggi and an Indian swami.

Before you could say Harrods, the book was withdrawn (temporarily at least) by its publishers, Century Hutchinson: but this only increased the author's frustration. He was one Steven Martindale and his swami introduced Pamella, a former Miss India, to Kashoggi and Mohamed Al Fayed and Martindale was always bumping into her with the Kashoggi set. He found her so boring that he did not bother to put her in his book. She found him so unrich that she did not bother to put him in her life. Sadly, he died this year.

Peregrine Worsthorne could surely have more finely polished his bleat in the *Sunday Telegraph* about the standards of the great editors of yesteryear who were always first on to Oxford High Tables or into European chancelleries. He might have pointed out that now they not only have to be first on to Pamella Bordes but also first into Port Stanley.

THE SPECTACLE OF Roland Rivron sawing the Bishop of Durham in half was one of the features of Paul Jackson's 'Ten Glorious Years' a BBC comedic celebration of Mrs Thatcher's regime to which I was most looking forward. Having anticipated being shipped to Liverpool to record this television epic, we finished up at Elstree. Quite rightly, the producers decided that to take ten spoof Thatchers (including one in bondage gear) to Merseyside, on the day that the lady was there herself sharing the grief of the Hillsborough victims and their relatives, would not be well judged. So we were back at what felt like a ghost town – the old ABC Elstree studios, where I made three Frankie Howerd 'Up' films (*Up Pompeii, Up The Chastity Belt* and *Up The Front* – a First World War epic) for the nation's cinematic treasure-house.

There were some cuts in the Thatcher tribute. For reasons of time Howard Goodall's dance *scena* ('When you're a wet you're a wet') had to go from his mini-musical *Marguerita!* (written with Rob Grant and Doug Naylor). I regret the loss of:

> When you're a wet
> It's a pretty safe bet
> That you're likely to end up
> A bitter back bencher for life.

But Gareth Smook's characterization of Alf Roberts purposeful 'sperm with a perm' which originated the Thatcher years gained depth with every rehearsal. 'I've no need for subtle tactics – I can puncture prophylactics – I'm the sperm!' he sang.

Alistair Beaton and I were allowed to resurrect some numbers from our Gilbert and Sullivan perversions on the South Bank for a music-hall return to Victorian Values. The Saatchis returned: 'We're *molto felici, siamo amici*, the future looks peachy for Saatchi and me!' A chorus of upwardly mobile Tory MPs were on parade in 'Tan Tan Tara': 'Loudly let the accents fray ...' The Chancellor's nightmare (sung by Doug Fisher) was:

> You dream there's some bleeder
> In league with the leader
> To elbow you out of your heaven
> You are under attack
> Then you're given the sack
> And Cecil's at No 11.

Neil Kinnock (Martin Connor) was there as 'The very Master of the multipurpose metaphor ... my language is poetical and full of hidden promises/it's like the raging torrent of a thousand Dylan Thomas's'; and Mrs Thatcher herself (Gaye Brown) was

Privatizing sewage
Though it's going to lose me votes
Because I'm very keen on selling anything that floats.

I AM WORRIED about the Palace of Westminster. Are they turning the Houses of Parliament into a theme park or a leisure centre or something? I went along to a reception hosted by Edward Taylor, MP, to celebrate the publication of *Margaret Thatcher; The Woman Within* by Andrew Thomson, her erstwhile political agent in Finchley. I think I might not have attended this junket had I not felt a responsibility to readers and publisher alike; but a sense of duty has always been my guiding light.

I was dropped off, as instructed, at the St Stephen's entrance (no parking facilities available) at a polite arrival time, 7.30 (7pm to 9pm the invitation said). We were bidden to the Westminster Hall Annexe. I know William Rufus built this hall – I'm not sure about the annexe, although I dare say that he would have approved what was going on there. Elizabeth Longford has reminded us in her new *Oxford Book of Royal Anecdotes* how suspect he was – habitually attended by hordes of 'pathics' and long-hairs wearing shoes with pointed toes.

Anyway, in the first annexe, which I entered by mistake, there were some very rum goings-on. A lot of people in psychedelic shirts (an adjective I haven't used since the '60s) were holding the Tennessee Darts Contest; not, I would have thought, a major function of the Mother of Parliaments.

Having made my excuses and left, I heard a braying noise along a corridor that might easily have led me to the woman within. Once inside the crowded chamber, I caught a brief glimpse of David Mellor and thought I had struck gold; but a suspicious young woman approached, fighting her way through lots of grey- and pin-stripe-suited youngish men. She looked at me accusingly. 'Are you,' I asked, 'celebrating ten years of Mrs Thatcher?'

'Certainly not,' she replied firmly. 'We are the Bow Group.'

Again I made my excuses, looked at my invitation and found it was a week hence.

I did go back the following Tuesday and found a much more decorous assembly. By 7.30pm there was no sign of our host, Teddy Taylor, and I could not spot the woman within or, indeed, any other MPs of the right or the left. The modest author was periodically hustled off through the thirsty hacks to address a camera or a microphone. I had a look at the book and you can take it from me that it was unlikely to cause much controversy.

IT IS NOT often that I'm invited to address the people of the United States of America, but when I am it is usually on some state occasion or in a time of national crisis. In 1977 I obliged for the ABC network on the subject of the Queen's jubilee. On the arrival of the Princess Beatrice (then unnamed), CBS invited me to speculate on what she would be called. Alas, I got no nearer than Sharon or Tracy. Then it was the turn of the CNN network (was it state occasion or national crisis?) which suggested that I should level with Americans on the subject of Mrs Thatcher and her ten years of leadership.

I prepared immediately beforehand by going to Mrs Winston Churchill's cocktail party for her husband's book, *Memories and Adventures*. Speak to a Churchill, I thought, and you will speak for England.

I met two enchanting ladies at the party, both, I think, in their eighties, who had been Sir Winston's secretaries. They had one worry, a matter in which I hope the readers can help. They would love to see again a three-minute film of Sir Winston talking to a robin by a bird bath in the gardens at Chartwell. They know that it was given to the Royal Airforce Volunteer Reserve, but since then it would seem to have disappeared. Short of writing to Jimmy Savile, I can think of no other way to retrieve it. (But later, thanks to a reader, we did).

I bumped into Michael Heseltine, whom I have hardly seen (to bump into, that is, his public profile has not been low)

since we both left Oxford. Here, I thought, was leadership, albeit waiting in the wings. Thinner than I remember, and a lot thinner than me, his hair shorter than the locks that once crowned a famous flak jacket, he offered me a lift, but no advice on how to present Mrs T to the Yanks.

When I got to CNN's premises in central London I found them informal, to say the least. A camera had been tripoded between the desks in the cluttered deserted office. Behind the chair in which I was to sit was a cloth splattered with paint squiggles, a sort of London scene as it might have been imagined by Utrillo, having a go at a Venetian skyline. The three CNN people thought it was much better than their previous backdrop. In spite of news breaking in Washington about the Oliver North verdict, we started bang on time (8.30 here, six hours earlier in Atlanta). Since I kept talking for the full ten minutes projected, I was assured it must have gone all right. You won't want to know what I said about the Prime Minister; but I did have one moment of abject insecurity when I was trying to draw a parallel with American politics. I mentioned the Democrats and then my mind blanked and I could not remember the name of their opponents. The only course seemed to be to wave away the entire Republican party with a lordly disregard and a muttered: 'You know – the others.'

It is reassuring to recall that on the momentous night when the world mourned John Kennedy's death, a Catholic priest arrived to deliver the epilogue on BBC television. His message was put on autocue, and after he had rehearsed it he was seen to be scribbling on a piece of paper. On transmission he delivered the scripted epilogue, and added the Lord's Prayer at the end. When he had left the studio, the staff saw that what he had written were the words of that prayer – lest he forgot, presumably.

I WAS INTRIGUED by a sale at Christie's, where '65 unpublished letters from Lillie Langtry, mistress of King Edward VII', were left unsold. According to *The Times*'s Sarah Jane Checkland, they were to 'Arthur Henry Jones, Mrs Langtry's secret lover ... saleroom experts could not explain why these *billets doux*, estimated at £15,000, attracted no real interest.'

I assumed that this was in fact Henry Arthur Jones, a playwright in the shadow of Pinero, who had a cockney accent. When he finished reading, as was the fashion, a new play to Mrs Patrick Campbell, she said: 'A very long play, Mr Jones, even without the aitches.'

I have some very small knowledge of Edwardian memorabilia and so I was not at all surprised they didn't fetch £15,000. Years ago I was planning a film about the king's later romance with Daisy, Countess of Warwick. Their correspondence came up for sale at Sotheby's. I paid £110 for a treasure trove of letters which whizzed between Arthur du Cros, MP (who was keen to bail out the royals), the Lords Stamfordam and Albemarle, courtiers, and the lawyers Charles Russell and Sir Henry Paget-Cooke.

There were also some intriguing accounts of expenses incurred by Lady Warwick on the back of Parisian hotel bills. One hundred thousand pounds in all, including her debts to

'Jews and Carters – £48,000'; and 'exactly £6,000 which I owe as a debt of honour to a friend'.

I also have Edward's love letters addressed with variations, to 'my own lovely, darling, little Daisy'. For keen students of drama at Chatsworth (according to the *earlier* theatrically minded Prince Edward), they include this excerpt, 'Mrs W James and Mr Leo Trevor acted a short impromptu piece. It was most amusing as the former impersonated a little girl of 12 in short petticoats and did it to perfection, whilst the latter got himself up as a schoolmistress and was remarkably clever ... They would make their fortunes on the stage ... It makes a welcome change from gambling.' His preferred sign-off was to 'my own adored little Daisy wife'.

I exaggerate when I say I have the letters. I have the transcripts. The originals were destroyed as part of the deal with the Palace before the posthumous scandal could erupt: but not before they were photographed on the glass plates used at the time. These plates were in Lot 661 as well.

At St James's Palace I dealt with Michael Adeane, grandson of Lord Stamfordam and his successor as private secretary to the monarch. He forecast no Palace objection to the subject, or perhaps he supposed correctly that the film would never be made. Some time after my plans had foundered, Coral Browne was announced in a West End play based on the same scandal. I asked her to dinner to look over the evidence. Another guest was my friend Canon Brian Brindley.

After dinner we got all the papers out and examined them on the floor. At one point Brian got up and strode across the room. Oblivious, he crushed the glass plates under his heel.

If anyone is adept at piecing together very small pieces of glass I have a modest commission for him; they might not make £15,000, but I'm sure they're worth more than a few old love letters to 'Enery Harthur, who was 'no Pinero', even if Shaw did prefer his plays.

Mary Malcolm, Lillie Langtry's granddaughter, took me to task about my rash assumption of the identity of her grandmother's secret lover. He was not the turn-of-the-century playwright. 'Arthur Henry', wrote Miss Malcolm, 'was an undistinguished Jersey man with a house at Portelet Bay who had loved my grandmother since they were both children. He had no money – and neither had she – but they loved one another through thick and thin and sundry scandals all their lives. He asked to be buried beside her and so he is.

'The letters, some of which I read at Christie's before the sale, were very touching indeed and gave me an insight into the real, unknown Lillie – a desperate woman trying to pay Ned Langtry's drink bills in London and writing to Jones of her dreams of a house in Portelet Bay, which they would share. The letters are full of instructions for planting the garden and news of boxes of plants being sent from England. I would have loved to have bought them.'

I think the unsuccessful vendors should give Mary custody.

I HAVE BECOME an art patron. In my hall I have a collection of some twenty-five glass sticks which I inherited from Caryl Brahms. They are charming, multicoloured, sugary things, twisted into shepherds' crooks and drum majors' batons: in a wilder fancy there is a bugle, and the pair Christopher Fry gave Caryl are glass duelling swords. She collected most of her sticks just after the war in Bristol. They began life as the offerings of Nailsea apprentices to their masters when they finished their indentures. Alongside them hang my decorative Marie Lloyd songsheets. In between stood the particularly ugly back of my front door.

Now the door is also hung with Marie Lloyd prints and glass sticks, and I can slam it as hard as I like without breaking them.

The answer is *trompe-l'oeil* and the magician who has brought off this eye-cheating trick is one Peregrine Elliot. I came across his work in the houses and restaurants of friends. He is following in the footsteps of Zeuxis and Parrhasius, two Greeks who, 2,400 years ago, played the mean trick of painting fruit so realistic that birds came to peck at it. Another legendary deception was the 'Unswept Floor', now in the Lateran Museum in Rome. This mosaic is the debris of a feast – chicken bones, pieces of cake and fruit rinds, each with its careful shadow, so that the whole floor is one ambitious deceit. In England, apart from Thornhill's magnificent Painted Hall in Greenwich, the fancy went chiefly to painting dead game birds and letter racks crammed with taped documents. I used to admire the late Martin Battersby's work and more recently those early James Bond book jackets *tromped* by Richard Chopping. My Man in Deal told me he thought the most notable contemporary examples are Graham Rust's murals at Fairlawn, Kent, done in 1985 – but this could just be Kentish pride.

He also tracked down a contemporary of Peregrine's, Sally Miles, who was commissioned by the Sultan of Brunei to add *trompe-l'oeil* to the splendours of his new palace. For the Sultan's favourite son she has conjured up a jungle vista, another room boasts an alpine view and a bedroom crowds in a castle manned by King Arthur's knights.

As patrons the Sultan and I are setting an example which the Cabinet could well follow. How pleasant if Nigel Lawson had handed over his Dorneywood dining room to Geoffrey Howe complete with fake groaning boards and a composition of his favourite fish and chips loosely wrapped in *The Times*. Howe could then commission from Peregrine or Mrs Miles a complementary collage of long unopened law books, bottles of Mogadon and a savaged dead sheep. Down at Chevening, John Major can ape Duke Gonzago of Mantua in the fourteenth century. He got Mantegna to turn a flat ceiling into a balconied dome opened at the top to a blue sky with people looking over the balustrade of the balcony. Major should strike a family note and go one better with his aerialist forebears tightroping and trapezing happily above his hall.

Chequers will be the decorative jewel in the Elliot-Miles crown. A convincing nineteenth hole would do for Denis's quarters: but Mrs T deserves to return from her holidays to find her own *trompe*. I suggest a Grantham grocer's counter with scales and a big till, packets of Typhoo Tea, jars of boiled sweets, the works.

It is odd the way different prime ministers regard Lord Lee of Fareham's bequest. Mrs T is always nipping off to Chequers. Harold Macmillan hardly stayed there at all – perhaps because Lady Dorothy didn't hit it off with the butch WAAF sergeant in charge of catering at the time. Macmillan installed Selwyn Lloyd there, except for one weekend when President Eisenhower dropped in. In the ensuing panic someone found out that for the entertainment of a head of state, protocol required the presence of the Lord Lieutenant of the county. Who was he? After a diligent search he proved to be the Earl of Buckinghamshire, a backwoodsman who had to be flown in from his seat in Scotland to kosher the occasion. His one exchange with the President was, 'Do ye shoot?' Eisenhower, doubtfully, 'Yes.' Earl: 'Grouse?' Eisenhower, emphatically: 'No.' Earl: 'Good God!' and that was the extent of his conversation.

IT WAS THE first time I had observed the Labour Party at the seaside. Its conference opened with a surprise – a theme from *Phantom of the Opera* by the Master of Tory Music. Otherwise it was business as expected. From my window each day before breakfast I could see the hallowed photo opportunities at the edge of the water on the beach, but this year no leader fell in. Hanging about the lobby of the Grand Hotel on Monday I spotted Roy Hattersley going to lunch (where else?); Robin Cook perched on one leg like a snoozing pink flamingo; Lord Longford looking lost; and Barbara Castle making the entrance of a theatrical dame – less imperious than Dame Edith, less vigorous than Dame Sybil, closer to Dame Anna Neagle in one of her frail but courageous roles. Odette Churchill, perhaps topped off with the red hair of Dame Anna's more skittish Nell Gwynn.

After Kinnock's speech on Tuesday the mood changed.

Suddenly the lobby filled out and the Grand was hosting a moderately successful first night – notices still not out. Jim Callaghan came up from the farm, John Prescott took his lighter image for a stroll, and Gerald Kaufman, Labour's entertainment buff, complained that there was no new musical or movie in town apart from *Sex, Lies and Videotape*, which he slyly compared to any party conference.

Kaufman, like John Smith, was surrounded by a fleet of aides murmuring, 'Yes, Shadow Minister.' Peter Shore sidled to the bar for a lager as Keith Waterhouse and I were sharing some bubbles. He muttered pettishly: 'Some people have something to celebrate, others just drink champagne.'

I hailed a retired BBC man down to do a little light interviewing as 'Robin Day, the writer'. 'Author,' he corrected, which prompted the journalist, David Bradley, to recall a Blackpool conference five years ago when the new knight told an old story. Sir Robin's opening sentence had been: 'A man said to me, "Mr Day", as I then was ...'

I was concerned there might be scandal after one lunch, when a delegate at the next table ordered *prostituto e melone*; but he will do well at the Foreign Office if Labour exceeds its expectations.

In 1905, looking down on the House of Commons, a friend of Keir Hardie remarked how few members of the working class sat below. 'Yes,' said Hardie, 'it will take the British working man twenty years to learn to elect his equals to represent him. And it will take him another twenty years not to elect his equals.'

Eighty-four years on, the platform array brought to mind something Attlee said in 1964 when he filmed an interview for the old 'Tonight' programme; off camera he remembered, 'Looking round the Cabinet table one day I said, "It's fortunate you don't have to appear on television, you're an ugly lot."' Loquacious for Attlee; but some things don't change.

I COLLECTED A couple of tales, political and royal, on my travels. The first is American, a Coolidge story.

The President and his wife were visiting a government farm. Passing the chicken coops, Mrs Coolidge enquired how often the rooster made love each day. 'Dozens of times,' was the reply. 'Please tell that to the President,' she said. When he passed the pen and was told about the rooster, he asked, 'Same hen every time?' 'Oh no, Mr President, a different one each time.' Coolidge nodded slowly. 'Please tell that to Mrs Coolidge.'

The royal report comes from Field Marshal Lord Carver's autobiography. Carver had an eccentric friend, one 'Loony' Hinde. King George VI was inspecting troops in North Africa in 1943. He put a routine question to Brigadier Hinde. 'Have we met before?' 'I don't think so,' said Hinde. 'You should bl ... bloody well know,' said the King tartly.

I SUPPOSE I MUST take the television of the House of Commons seriously, so I tried out the invaluable SIPS, the Sherrin Interview Poll System. These are the results of a poll conducted (after a good lunch) with several people into whom I happened to bump in the King's Road, Chelsea.

63 per cent said that seeing MPs as well as hearing them made them more, rather than less boring.

47 per cent said it was not as good as 'Neighbours'.

11 per cent (mainly children) said they took fright on seeing Mrs Thatcher in close-up. One Conservative voter thought she looked better on 'Spitting Image'.

7 per cent admired Mr Speaker's wig. One very odd chap said that he always thought Sir Robin Day *was* the Speaker.

8 per cent complained they could not see the MP who always says 'Yah, Yah' in the background.

5 per cent wanted to know which was Mr Hattersley's favourite restaurant and who was Mr Lawson's dietician.

3 per cent asked the name of Mr Heseltine's barber.

2 per cent (mostly Japanese) had never heard of the House of Commons.

1 per cent (an Eskimo tourist) had never heard of television.

During the excerpts that I viewed there was, surprisingly, little discussion of the economy. But John Major might like to consider the latest evidence of galloping inflation to hand. Last week my friend Neil Shand overheard two well-dressed men raising their voices in Ebury Street, Pimlico. 'We shouldn't be arguing about a mere 25,000 quid,' shouted one.

A few years ago it would have been: 'It's only a fiver, squire.'

SIR ANTHONY MEYER'S challenge to Mrs Thatcher reminded me of a more famous, if equally unrewarding, occasion. In July 1942, a critical time for Winston Churchill's war leadership, an influential back-bencher, Sir John Wardlaw-Milne, opened a debate censuring the Prime Minister.

Things looked shaky for Churchill until, half-way through his damaging speech, Sir John suddenly suggested that the King's brother, the Duke of Gloucester, a most unlikely choice, be made Commander-in-Chief of the British forces. The House fell about.

In the words of Harold Nicolson, 'his influence was shattered'. Churchill got his vote of confidence by 476 to 25. Perhaps the Chief Whip should suggest to Sir Anthony that he lobbies for Princess Michael of Kent as the next leader of the Tory party.

I HAD BULGARIA on my mind as the domino effect hit the Balkans. Were we going to embrace the Bulgars as enthusiastically as we were turning on to Poles, East Germans, Hungarians and Czechs? Would names like Mladenov, Alexandrov and Zhivkov soon fit happily on our lips? Should we forget Georgi Markov murdered with a poisoned umbrella?

Perhaps the most sympathetic Bulgarian was King Boris the Sociable. In 1936 he was shocked to read in John Gunter's *Inside Europe* that he was 'the worst dressed king in Europe' because, for patriotic reasons, he insisted on wearing clothes made in Sofia. He changed immediately to Savile Row.

Many of his predecessors were less amiable, Khan Krum, who was in charge during the ninth century, slew the invading Nicephoros and converted his skull into a drinking goblet by lining it with silver – a design concept Sir Terence Conran might care to adopt.

An impressionable successor, Khan Boris, was terrified into better behaviour by pictures of hell painted on his palace walls by crafty Byzantine monks. But in 1014, Tsar Samuel was defeated by a northern invader, Bazil II, known as the Slayer of the Bulgars, who put out the eyes of 15,000 prisoners.

Do we need a *rapprochement* with these people?

Even the name is tainted. *Bulgaris* in Latin was synonymous with perversion and when, in 1223, the French Catholic hierarchy accused the Albigensian heretics (who came from Eastern Europe) of the same thing, they called them *Bougres*; hence a popular modern English epithet.

It used to be said that every private soldier in the Bulgarian army carried a field marshal's lipstick in his knapsack. Can we trace this slur to Evelyn Waugh? During the Second World War Waugh was reluctantly appointed ADC to a general whose company he did not relish. He took to the bottle and, inspired by wine, asked the old boy if he was aware that in the Bulgarian army only officers of field rank were allowed to wear lipstick. He was instantly relieved of his post.

There are other reasons for keeping the Bulgars at arm's length. Are we likely to learn much from their art? The most famous play by Vasil Drumov ('The Father of the Bulgarian Theatre') is called *An Unhappy Family*. It does not sound like a barrel of laughs to me.

Nor does the latest Bulgarian joke. 'Have you heard about the economical mousetrap which works without cheese? The mouse shakes its head in disgust and cuts its throat on a saw.' One for Frank Carson?

LAST CHRISTMAS I addressed myself to the problem of finding stocking fillers. What would you get for the great and the good?

For John Major: pips that squeak.

For Geoffrey Howe: a party hat that stays on.

Douglas Hurd: a rubber duck.

Cecil Parkinson: a high-speed train set.
Neil Kinnock: a second prize.
Roy Hattersley: a second helping.
The Speaker: earplugs.
Paddy Ashdown: a few 'doughnuts' to give the illusion of a party.

Dennis Skinner: a pair.
Nicholas Ridley: an ashtray.
Gordon Brown: a touch of the DTIs.
Tony Benn: an endless tape.
Eric Heffer: Keir Hardie's cap.
And for Mrs Thatcher: a phrase book that translated the word 'No' into every European language.

IN HELPFUL MOOD as the year closed, I was concerned for the unemployed. Not our 1.5 million Brits, but all those heads of government who had lost their jobs or might see them go in the near future. Rajiv Gandhi could return to the Boeings as a pilot: 'This is your ex-prime minister speaking, we are now flying at 35,000 feet.' But he would have to remember to go on: 'Fasten your seat belts,' and not, 'Fill in your voting cards.'

Ronald Reagan could do that final remake of *Casablanca*, for which he was cast in the first place.

To East Germany's former leader, Erich Honecker, formerly
a communist youth leader, I could only wish an unhappy
second childhood. Ceausescu was no longer my responsibility,
nor was ex-president Husak (Czechoslovakia), formerly a
lawyer, who would be fully occupied looking for a very good
one indeed.

General Pinochet should revert to square-bashing rather
than peon-bashing.

If Mrs Thatcher fails to win next time, she has two possi-
bilities. Will it be a Nobel Prize as a research chemist –
'Duchess of Belton discovers the elixir of life' – or will it be
glory and silk at the Bar – 'I don't care how the jury voted, I
am a majority of one'?

A final thought for Captain Bob Maxwell. How about being
the next King of Albania? What is going to happen in Albania –
the last Red domino to fall? Who else could lead them to
glasnost and *perestroika*? Is there an available descendant of
the national hero, George Castriota? Known as 'Skandesberg',
in 1443 he expelled the ruling Turks. To Byron he was 'Iskan-
der' in *Childe Harold*.

Benevolent leadership has been a problem recently. In 1912
C B Fry, the England cricketer, was offered the throne. Prince
William of Wied lasted two years. Ahmed Zog, in a record
ascent, was PM in 1922, President in 1925, and King Zog the
One (and Only) in 1928. In the 1930s Mussolini tried to marry
him to an Italian princess. She plumped for Boris of Bulgaria.
Zog finally married a Hungarian, Geraldine, before fleeing
Il Duce's troops. Their heir, who is incredibly tall, lives in
South Africa with an Australian wife who answers the phone
saying: 'The King is out, Queen Susan speaking.' Recently,
the official *New Albanian Magazine* commend the late John
Belushi, an American-born ethnic Albanian, as a 'classical
beauty ... sincere, loving, and devoted to his wife'. That
was all wide of the mark, but Belushi's brother Jim might be
a candidate.

In the Fry tradition, I recommend an English cricketer
poet for king. Why not Tim Rice? One day the phone in the

palace in Tirana might be answered by Queen Elaine: 'Don't cry for me, dear Albania.'

In Moscow, a member of the Congress of People's Deputies was enthusing recently about the pace of change, 'especially now we have our women's group'. My man in Moscow thought he was in on the first stirrings of feminism inside the Soviet Union. 'We are sending them to classes,' said his proud informant. 'We were so embarrassed by our wives. They don't know how to eat, which knife, which fork, what to do with a napkin. They don't know how to dress to dance ... the women's group is now making great progress.' So much for Russian feminism.

From Budapest, my man reported a curious legacy of Husak. The President had a peculiar passion for bathrooms. All his official buildings are splattered with them. Now that a new and more enlightened bureaucracy is evolving, you cannot walk down those corridors of power without seeing secretaries squatting on bathtubs hammering at their typewriters, which are perched precariously on washbasins.

THE YEAR OF 1990 could have been a monstrous one for anniversaries. Fifty years earlier Germany invaded Holland and Belgium, Churchill became Prime Minister, there was Dunkirk, France fell, the Blitz began and that's only half of it. Fifty years earlier still Eisenhower was born and it was his centenary which Lord Stockton celebrated at the Festival Hall in the first week of June with assorted sons and grandsons of Eisenhower, Churchill, Alexander and Montgomery as well as British and American big bands, revered singing stars and the music of Ike's period.

We had breakfast at the Hyde Park Hotel to talk about the event. Stockton was quickly diverted into anecdotage. He met Eisenhower twice. On the second occasion, when the general was very old, Alexander complimented him on his autobiography. 'It's wonderful,' he said to the aged former President. 'So they tell me,' agreed Ike amiably.

Alexander also had two good Churchill stories. Suddenly and unusually flush after the publication of his *History of the English Speaking Peoples*, he worried about how much he could leave his children after death duties. Randolph suggested a scheme by which Winston would write an article libelling him in a Beaverbrook newspaper. Beaverbrook would be indemnified. Randolph would then collect the loot and death duties would be avoided. 'A brilliant plan, Randolph,' intoned the great man. 'I see only one problem. Nothing I could write about you could possibly stand up as libel in a court of law.'

There was also a sweet, sad tale of Churchill immediately after the resignation which followed his stroke. He gave his Cabinet the news. As they left he sat alone, dejected, in the Cabinet Room. Norman Brook, the Cabinet Secretary, came in and, seeing his head bowed, carried a crumb of comfort. 'Prime Minister,' he said, 'you know that you and Colonel X were the only two survivors of the last great cavalry charge, the one at Omdurman.' Churchill nodded. 'I have to tell you sir, that Colonel X died yesterday. You are the sole survivor.' Churchill raised his head. 'How uncommonly civil of him,' he said.

While working at the Nuffield Theatre I picked up a happy piece of local history in Southampton, the scene of one of the war's remarkable mini-dramas. On 2 June 1944, Churchill was there in his personal train, determined to accompany the invasion forces on D-Day (6 June).

For safety reasons, Eisenhower and the service chiefs were equally determined to prevent him. They played a desperate card. That evening, Churchill received a message from George VI saying that if it was right for the Prime Minister to take part in the invasion, then he himself had an even stronger claim as head of all three fighting services. Churchill gave in.

THE REVELATION THAT the Queen, with an estimated personal fortune of £2.4 billion, is the richest woman in the world had about the same impact as the news that Christmas comes but once a year. After all, she paid no death duties on the demise of George VI and she has subsequently paid no income tax on her personal investments, and quite right.

It was not always so. In 1842 Queen Victoria volunteered to pay income tax. Edward VII continued this practice. When George V succeeded in 1910 he was informed by the government (who had consulted Sir Rufus Isaac, the Solicitor-General), that he need not subscribe. In return he offered to contribute to the cost of state visits out of his civil list money. He also generously chipped in £100,000 towards the cost of the First World War – which must have bought a few more howitzers than it would today. He later took an economy cut in the civil list during the depression from 1931 to 35. In 1948 King George VI also handed back £100,000 saved from the civil list during the Second World War. At least they didn't have Prince Edward's hassle. A London evening pa~er rang me to ask if he was homosexual. I could only say that he hadn't made a pass at me.

EVER WILLING TO help the Prime Minister, and even the Leader of the Opposition, I have a suggestion to replace their respective unpopular poll and roof taxes. Bring back the window tax. Think of the revenue to be gained from the hideous Department of the Environment building or Centrepoint. Hard luck, I suppose, on Chatsworth and its famous Tudor neighbour, 'Hardwick Hall, more glass than wall'.

William of Orange cooked up the original idea in 1695 to make up the usual deficiency in the Exchequer caused on that occasion by sharp lads who had chipped and defaced silver coins. The tax was imposed on buildings with more than six windows. I've counted mine and I have nine. If you had between ten and nineteen it cost you four shillings. In its first year the window tax yielded the impressive sum of £1,200,000. It survived until 1851, and there is one aspect of its history which will strike a chord in Mrs Thatcher's breast. In 1774 there is a reference to 'the Collector of the Window-lights in Falkland's Island'.

There's Nothing Like a Dame

I saw Bette Davis during her 1987 visit to London. There are not many 79-year-old ladies who, having had, in the past five years or so, a mastectomy, a stroke and a broken hip, could throw a corps of show business reporters into nervous disarray and bring the public out on the streets in thousands. When Miss Bette Davis 'hit town', it was a little as though the circus had arrived – the media circus. She had a practice run at Deauville before she invaded Britain. By the time I got to see her in the Harlequin Suite on the fifth floor of the Grosvenor House Hotel I had read her new book, *This 'N That*, and reminded myself of her movie highs and lows from *Mother Goddam*, a biography by Whitney Stine which she annotated with devastating personal comments in bright red print. I had also seen her on 'Wogan' looking frail, but deftly controlling her chubby interrogator with imperious formality.

I had met Miss Davis once before, I think about fifteen years previously, at a cocktail party given by Joan Bakewell when the Star was to answer questions at the NFT under Joan's chairpersonship. I didn't get much animation out of her then until I made my excuses and left because I was off to dinner at Rex Harrison's – a name which struck a chord. Some years later I asked her to be in a film I was hoping to produce with her and Glenda Jackson and Michael York. Her agent showed interest, indeed enthusiasm; but (my fault) I failed to raise the money.

On this occasion the time fixed for me to talk to The Living Legend was changed three times by her publicist. We switched from 6 on a Friday evening to 4 and then back to 5. By a happy chance, I was lunching at the Grosvenor House that day, and on the way out I found a journalist who had already run into my Star that day. She was still signing books at Hatchards, he said. He painted a daunting picture of Miss Davis surrounded by three thousand fans of all ages, all clamouring for her to put her name and a brief message on their copies of *This 'N That*. Sweat was apparently pouring down her face; and Hatchards had to lock the doors for safety. Police were controlling the crowds in Piccadilly.

What sort of woman, I wondered, was it who, at 79 (post mastectomy, stroke and hip fracture), could cope with this sort of afternoon and then chat happily to me for an hour? It was still only 3.30 so, musing apprehensively on this, I went on my way and came back an hour later. My new journalist friend was still there. Miss Davis had returned from Hatchards, he said, in a flurry of activity, declining to sign autographs for fans around the door, striding purposefully towards the lift, breathing fire and brimstone – and, when he had slipped into the lift with her, scattering unflattering remarks about former acting colleagues like grape-shot.

I prepared to meet a tired and tetchy old lady, I phoned her suite at 4.55, and promptly at five o'clock I was told by her assistant to present myself. The assistant was Kathryn Sermak, an extremely attractive American girl who featured prominently in *This 'N That* as the guardian angel who saw Miss Davis through all her illnesses. Behind her, as she opened the door to the suite, I could see The Star puffing on a characteristic cigarette. Immaculately presented in a stylish chocolate dress with yellow spots and pearls and showing no sign of fan damage, she politely pretended to remember our previous meeting: but not the projected film; and settled down patiently to answer the same questions she had been asked all week.

Bette Davis was very businesslike, very crisp, direct and correct. Whether she was remembering with gratitude and affection George Arliss, who gave particular help and good advice over fifty years earlier in the shaky early days of her career, or recalling with irritation the exasperating conduct of Faye Dunaway on a recent film in which they appeared together, it was always 'Mr Arliss' and 'Miss Dunaway'. With the exception of Mr Quentin Crisp, I have never met anyone who punctuates their conversation with the words 'Mr', 'Mrs' or 'Miss' more frequently than Miss Davis. Get them chatting together and the air would swoon with sibilants.

There are so many famous Bette Davis stories, and she has told them so often, that one tries to avoid the subjects that make her glaze over with boredom. She'd had two television interviews earlier in the week. One girl had asked 'nothing new', and the other had wasted twenty minutes out of the thirty reading out Miss Davis's horoscope to her. However, she lit up at the mention of her first visit to England in 1936 when she was on the run from an iniquitous Warner Bros film contract, and had had to face Sir Patrick Hastings, KC, in court. She launched into a spirited imitation of Sir Patrick's sarcastic opening remarks and his petulance when he realized that he was not going to have a chance to cross-examine her. Surprisingly, she did not know that he had gone on to become a successful playwright. I got the impression that she might have relished the chance to turn down one of his scripts!

I asked if she thought the public wanted to hear about her as survivor actress, wife or mother. Her book contains a brief reply to an earlier attack by her daughter, B D Hyman – *My Mother's Keeper* – but everyone talking to Miss Davis had been given strict instructions that any mention of daughter or book would lead to immediate termination of the interview, so a reference to her role as 'mother' was as near the wind as I allowed myself to sail. I was not surprised that she chose to talk about surviving. She feels that the triumphant story of her 'complete recovery from these illnesses would encourage others, particularly those weak and helpless with strokes, to believe in the possibility of overcoming the inevitable handicaps'.

It was in June 1983 that she had her mastectomy. Nine days

later the stroke followed, and her big battle with herself and
the hospital staff began. Miss Davis has a clear perception of
how the nursing staff viewed her – as a challenge. They looked
forward to going home nightly and boasting to their nearest
and dearest that they had told Bette Davis what to do and
where to get off. There is no doubt that Bette's life was in
danger; but so I should imagine was the life of the nurse who
on one occasion 'told me to say "please" when I asked her to
do something'. Stavros Niarchos, the Greek shipowner, must
also have been at risk. He donated ten million dollars to the
hospital and then demanded Miss Davis's room for his son
who had just broken his jaw. Miss Davis declined to move.
She and Kathryn Sermak made a formidable team with the
young girl saying, 'We'll make it,' or, 'We made it', at every
turning point – each operation, each step across the room, the
removal from hospital to hotel suite, the return home to
California, facing friends again and finally, starting to work
once more.

'Old age ain't no place for sissies' is the inscription on one
of Miss Davis's embroidered pillows, and sissies would be well
advised to keep away from her. She asked me if we still had a
problem getting staff in England. I explained that it didn't
weigh too heavily on me. The shortcomings of staff feature
heavily in Miss Davis's memories of her recovery. She had a
succession of cooks who brewed for themselves, not for her,
who hid food and wasted food and who brought in 'cookies'
which they claimed were home baked. One sinful girl even
tried to pass off some stuffed peppers in tomato sauce as her
own. Miss Davis had recovered enough to rummage in the
rubbish and find the manufacturer's wrapping. Those big eyes
were still not for having wool pulled over.

Bette Davis wrote *This 'N That* a little like our conversation.
She magpied about from hospital treatment to memories of
her long career. The news that Mrs Richard Nixon was in the
next ward set her off to remember, 'little Ronnie Reagan', and
how stuffy he became when he was Governor of California
and, at a Warner Bros reunion, required Edward G. Robinson,

Bette Davis, Bogart and Bacall and other bigger stars to stand in response to his entrance.

A mention of Hedda Hopper's dictum that she could always tell when Bette Davis was in love because there was a glow to her screen performances drew enthusiastic assent, and also a tribute to Miss Hopper's rival columnist, Louella Parsons, who 'looked so innocent and could sum anything up in a sentence'; and a disparaging remark about the girl the *Sunday Times* had sent to talk to her. 'You'd think a great paper like the *Times* could send someone responsible ... she kept asking the same question, ... why was I still acting in my old age ... did I need the money?' Reading the interview later, I saw the reporter had re-phrased it. 'Old age' became 'later years'. The girl had committed another sin which had not gone unnoticed. 'She'd never heard of Miss Lillian Gish.' (Bette Davis's co-star in *The Whales of August*.)

Miss Davis got back on the subject of on-screen glow and pointed out that you only had to look at her screen performances with George Brent and Gary Merril to recognize the incandescence that Hedda Hopper was writing about. I thought I'd risk an impertinent question and suggested that at 79 if this 'in-love glow' didn't happen again she might never give another decent performance. She laughed quite a lot at that, stubbed out a cigarette and said, conspiratorially, 'You're quite right. I'm finished.' Nobody ever looked less ready to give up.

We talked about the crush at her book signing. She was jubilant: 'Three thousand books and I signed every one.' Kathryn had told Hatchards to get some policemen to control the crowds. Hatchards had demurred. 'We've had Prince Andrew here, we didn't need police to control that.' Kathryn had insisted – fortunately; the chaos in Piccadilly was formidable. Both were impressed by the range of fans – elderly to punk. Punk dyed hair and mohican cuts seemed exotic to Kathryn. Miss Davis, who may have misjudged the sexual preferences of some of the lads, on account of their flamboyant plumage, explained, 'Most of those boys are, you know ... I have a lot of those fans. Judy Garland and I had the biggest following.... When I played the Palladium they thought they would have trouble selling out a night. I had to play a week to packed houses.... This particular type of fan was so emotional.... When I was doing my Carl Sandburg readings in New Orleans, I went up in the elevator with two of these boys and one of them fell in a dead faint at my feet.'

This looked like the perfect cue to tell my favourite Bette Davis story and see it if was true. I broached the idea and she settled down to listen. I asked her to interrupt if she recognized the tale. With those huge eyes opened unblinkingly, I set off.

Some years ago, two men in New York entered their apartment block and got into the elevator to find they were sharing it with Bette Davis – their screen idol. Their delight was doubled when they all got out on the same floor and they found that she was their new neighbour across the hall. Plucking up their courage, they asked her to dinner – she accepted for Friday at 7.30. Prompt and immaculate as ever, she arrived and they dined and talked until 11 when she said she must go to bed. As she left she returned their invitation for the next Friday at the same time. Their joy was unconfined. She went to great trouble to match their splendid meal and then at 11 indicated once again it was bed time. And according to my story, as they reached the door, she said, with the utmost finality, 'Well, now we've done *that*!'

This somewhat brutal termination of the friendship revealed to me a wonderful balance between elaborate old Yankee politeness and the determination of a strong woman not to encumber her life with more friends than she needed or sought.

Miss Davis and Kathryn scratched their heads for some time and compared notes. No, they could not recall any such circumstance ... no, they didn't think it could have happened. Wasn't it funny how stories like that built up? I was sad to have my myth destroyed; but maybe there's a higher truth lurking somewhere in the parable.

By the time I had finished the allotted hour – she insisted that she was not tired and that I must have my full quota – I was glad of the injunction not to talk about the daughter or the daughter's book. I'm sure Bette Davis can be regally demanding when she wishes, and especially when she feels she is being short changed; however, to me, she had been patient and courteous. In answer to her daughter in *This 'N That* (apart from memories of pleasant times together dotted through her book) she adds a short open letter at the end which contrives to be both sharp and moving. The strictest dig is the postscript. 'PS I hope some day I will understand the title *My Mother's Keeper*. If it refers to money, if my memory serves me right, I've been your keeper all these many years. I am continuing to do so, as my name has made your book about me a success.'

Somehow I didn't carry away the impression of a sad, lonely old lady. Miss Davis was still (to use an American word) *feisty*, proud of her capacity to fight back and proud of the adoration she still inspires in her fans; if any one could look after themselves, I should think it is she. Subsequently I asked her ex-agent about the dinner party story and its accuracy. 'Oh, yes,' he said, 'I remember the block and the boys.'

IT WAS GOOD to stroll around the old EMI lot at Elstree and to sit at my old table in the restaurant. My experiences with Zsa Zsa Gabor when she played Mati Hari there, opposite Frankie Howerd in *Up The Front*, came flooding back. The initial negotiations concerned travel, transport, accommodation and especially costume, make-up and hair. Zandra Rhodes, who was just making her reputation, designed two dresses for Zsa Zsa who purred her pleasure down the phone from Los Angeles and arrived in London on a Friday so that she could get over her jet lag and settle in to start shooting on the Monday.

We took her to the rooms she had specifically asked for in Piccadilly. The hotel welcomed her obsequiously and she examined her quarters imperiously. She found them wanting. It was the lack of hanging space that concerned her. She was shown another suite. To me it seemed identical. To Zsa Zsa it was perfect. 'You see, darlink, why do they not offer me this one first time?'

Intimations of trouble started halfway through Saturday. I had foolishly sent along a woman hair-dresser. Zsa Zsa packed

her off smartly and called me to coo that she had done so. 'She left very happy, darlink! I tell her she is a sweet girl; but not for me. But you do not have to worry, I have found this marvellous man. He is divine! He understands me. He works for my great friend ... [aside] What is his name? ... [to me] ... Ricci Burns!' Burns was a fashionable 60s King's Road crimper. I was about to explain that his chap would not be allowed to work at Elstree unless he was a member of the right union, when Zsa Zsa embarked on a perfectly shaped monologue.

'He is so good to me, this Ricci. He has sent me this beautiful man. The girl was nice but she did not understand me. This man is wonderful ... you are wonderful, darlink ...

he has done all the best people. I have complete confidence in him ... Tell me who you have done, darlink! I am talking to my producer, he would like to know. [To me] He cannot remember. [To him] You must have done someone ... Are you any good? ... I only have the best ... Are you *very* good? Me ...! Of course I am good ... You do not ask me this! How dare you say that! ... What? ... What is this? Clapped out! Go away! Get out! [Door bangs] Darlink, I do not think he will do. Do not worry, we will find someone better. *Au revoir!*'

We found her a union man and no more was heard of the hair problem. But by now she was ready to launch her attack on Zandra. 'Zandra is the best dressmaker in the world. *But!* ... and, darlink, she is so amusing, the green and pink hair and the funny accent ... *But!* ... and I am sure the clothes would be wonderful for someone else ... *But!*' She then revealed that she happened to have brought a pair of 'old rags' of her own – pink confections which I suspect she had intended to wear all along. She fascinated Zandra, who took the dismissal in her stride and begged to be concealed in the studio to study this exotic creature further at close quarters. Years later they met again in America and became friends.

Taking Zsa Zsa to a first night was an exercise fraught with danger. One evening, after she had had a late night out at Les Ambassadeurs and worked through the day from an early call, we drove in together from Elstree. On the way she developed a craving for a salt beef sandwich but we couldn't find one in the Finchley Road, not even for ready money. We got to the Globe Theatre – just in time for me to buy her a box of chocolates.

The play, written by Frank Marcus and directed by Robin Phillips, was earnestly acted by Nigel Davenport and Irene Worth, and it very soon drove Zsa Zsa into a deep and sleepy gloom. Soon her head began to sag. It is a large, pinkish-white head, and her shoulders were swathed in white fur. She had not dressed to be inconspicuous and she wasn't. We were sitting in front of the Rex Harrisons and the Carl Foremans and I had to invent a routine like Chaplin's in *Modern Times* to keep her upright.

As the big blonde head sagged, I would nudge her side. Her right hand then stretched out automatically, clutched a chocolate and stuffed it into her mouth. The effort, the munching and the sugar in the soft centres gave her a temporary lift; and her head snapped back into position. A few minutes later, down it went again, out stretched the arm, in went the hand and up went the chocolate and the head. There were just enough chocolates to see the ritual and the evening through.

GLEN ROVEN, THE American composer-lyricist, is a good gossip. Some years ago he took those two formidable musical queens, Ethel Merman and Ann Miller, on a weekend drive in Buck's County, Pennsylvania.

The natives were indulging in an orgy of car-boot sales. Merman, a tireless collector of jumble, strode up to the first stall, tended by two elderly musical-comedy enthusiasts. Recognizing their double catch, the two men were overcome and pleaded: 'Take anything you want, Miss Merman, Miss Miller. Don't think about paying.' Merman's eyes lit up, 'Annie,' she said, at her most commanding, 'go get a bag!'

Dame Ann Miller is an American icon. She does not owe her honour to the Queen but to the Order of St John and the Knights of Malta. The evidence is stowed in Dame Ann's large glass memorabilia cabinet in her large Beverly Hills home. It needs to be large (the cabinet), because Dame Ann has a lot of trophies to display. Beside Tony Award nominations and that sort of thing they include the Hall of Fame Award for Famous Legs and the Anti-Defamation League Award for being A Woman of Importance. On her walls hang framed cables from Ron and Nancy. 'They say I'm to the right of John Wayne. I don't understand it. I'm not political. Ronnie was a colleague.'

Anyone who saw her in the great MGM musicals with Sinatra and Kelly in *On The Town*, with Garland and Astaire in *Easter Parade* or with Howard Keel in *Kiss Me Kate* will know who Ann Miller is – a warm, friendly broad cast in the Merman mould but making her best effects with her legs not her larynx. When she was 67, she had been tapping her way around America for nine years in *Sugar Babies*, which was her first Broadway show for forty years. A big, bawdy, burlesque musical, noisy and funny, it alternated Dame Ann's tommy-gun style of tapping with a lot of girls and joyous, ancient, low-comedy routines exhumed by the show's deviser, Ralph

Allen. These were led by an exuberant Mickey Rooney. Dame Ann appears in some of the sketches, too, towering over Rooney, majestically detached from the confident vulgarity which surrounds her, giving not an inch.

America's attitude to her is somewhere between reverence for a national monument and affection for a national joke. She enjoys the joke, much of which is of her own making. It stems from her wig. Her jet-black hair stretches down to her waist but on stage it is tucked away under a stiff, heavily-lacquered half-wig. 'Ann Miller fell and broke her hair,' goes one crack; and a New York TV weathercaster was moved to say, 'There was a high wind in Manhattan today – a hair moved on Ann Miller's head.' One reason Dame Ann can see the joke is because in 1972, when she was opening a tour of *Anything Goes*, a steel curtain dropped on her skull. 'There was blood all over the stage, but there could have been more,' she says. 'This dumb wig saved my life.'

When I turned up at her handsome house she was finishing her regulation daily two hours of tap practice, providing iced tea and thinking about London (to which town she later brought the show). It also featured venerable variety performers. I asked about one old gentleman whose act was to eat everything in sight. 'I suppose he ate one shirt too many.' What about the disobedient dog act? 'I think the dog died.'

There is an over-used, over-sentimental American expression about 'paying your dues' (pronounced 'doos') which means earning your success. Dame Ann started early when her father, a criminal lawyer, parted from her near-deaf mother. (Born in Texas, her ancestry is French, Irish and Cherokee.) At eleven she was dancing (she'd trained since five to rectify rickets) at five dollars a night for an audience of Rotarians, Elks and Shriners. Mother told them that she was eighteen and perhaps they believed her. She made her first film in 1937 when she was fourteen, and mother had to fib again. The legacy of this piece of misinformation is that the reference books are divided about whether she was born in 1919 or 1923; I believe 1923. She was lucky in her film apprenticeship –

directed by George Cukor and playing with Katharine
Hepburn, Ginger Rogers and Lucille Ball in *Stage Door* and
she was very impressed by Miss Hepburn's habit of stopping
filming at four each day and ordering afternoon tea. (She
hoped this civilized practice would obtain when they rehearsed
Sugar Babies over here.) Then she played a ballet dancer for
Frank Capra in *You Can't Take it With You*. This time she
told them (incorrectly) that she had experience on point and
permanently damaged her toes in unblocked shoes.

At fifteen she was thrown to the Marx Brothers in *Room
Service*, and confronted on the first day by a Harpo who
promptly dropped his trousers. She shared an agent with
Eleanor Powell, who was preparing to hang up her tap shoes.
He sent Dame Ann to Broadway for the 1939 edition of *The
George White Scandals*. The show was not a success but Dame
Ann stopped it in a number called 'The Mexiconga'.

When she went back to Hollywood her weekly wage went
up from $250 a week to $3,000. Again she was lucky with a
great director, George Abbott, in an indifferent film, *Too
Many Girls*. She was also loaned out to appear with Rudy
Vallee and the cowboy star Gene Autry. 'I was the first girl he
kissed apart from his horse.'

She published her autobiography, *Miller High Life*, in 1972
and when I saw her was writing a second book, *Tapping into
the Force*, with Dr Thelma Moss, a hypnotist-regressionist
from UCLA. Here a rather different Dame Ann takes over
and if you are sceptical, as I am, you will simply have to go
along with me and take it from me, as I took it from her.
Her perception may be questioned but not her sincerity. Her
Cherokee grandmother was psychic. At an early age she
spotted signs of a similar gift in her granddaughter. Dr Moss
had visited Dame Ann with a little hypnotism in mind. Dame
Ann didn't 'hypnotize easy' and told her so. Three hours
later she woke up having apparently spent time regressing to
Ancient Egypt where, she explained, she and her sister had
been murdered by her half-brother. No specific names were
mentioned but Dame Ann is an old Egypt hand and long

ago she identified herself as Queen Hatshepsut in a previous incarnation. 'I was the only woman Pharaoh.' Apart from the regression with Dr Moss she had visited modern Egypt four times, and each time she caught some mysterious sickness. Only on the last occasion did she manage to get to Luxor and have a look at her tomb. She took one glance and announced, 'The body was never in that tomb.' Now, she told me, later evidence suggested that she may have uncannily hit the mark. Apparently her father's tomb was found to be severely over-crowded, with no fewer than three mummies in it. Emerging from the site, she was bitten by a scorpion 'or some such thing', and only saved by her guide and escort, Kamal al Malak, who threw himself at her feet and sucked the venom from her ankle. She still took some days to recover but the famous legs are unimpaired.

After such an exotic escapade it seemed an anticlimax to return to Dame Ann's American husbands. There have been three, all millionaires, all in oil. In *Kiss Me Kate* Cole Porter had her sing:

> There's an oilman known as Tex
> Who is keen to give me checks
> And his cheeks I fear
> Mean that sex is here – to stay!

All were unsatisfactory. In 1946 she married her first who, unknown to her, had a steel plate in his head which made him violent when drunk. After he had pushed her downstairs and provoked a miscarriage she called it a day. The next husband, vintage 1958, was also too keen on other vintages and once again she divorced him. In 1961 her mother introduced her to Arthur Cameron, who was nearer her mother's age, which did not stop him carrying on like a bachelor and that marriage was promptly annulled.

In an echo of Egypt she once dined with Lord 'Porchy' Carnarvon (son of the man who paid for the King Tut exca-vations) who asked her for an autographed photograph and, she had been told, always displayed it prominently at Highclere. She was not averse to a suitable English escort while she was here with *Sugar Babies* and seemed disappointed that the sixth Earl of Carnarvon was already spoken for.

One of her great triumphs in America was a very famous commercial for Great American Soups. In a whimsy of Stan Freeberg's she danced on top of an eight-foot soup can, encircled by twenty-foot water fountains, a 24-piece orchestra and an array of chorus girls. For a climax she tapped her way into the kitchen where her husband (fictional, not one of the millionaires) said, 'Why must you make such a big production out of everything?'

DRIVING THROUGH THE leafy Sussex lanes with Alexandra Bastedo, I was treated to riveting titbits from the autobiography she was writing. She was very funny about the courtship techniques of Warren Beatty, Steve McQueen and Omar Shariff. Mr McQueen's line, 'I asked you here as a woman, Alexandra', deserves a place in some anthology of overtures. And Beatty working his way through his phone book in the course of a night – he called Alexandra at about midnight and three hours later got round to her flatmate whose initial was S – qualifies him for an Oscar for persistence. Another theatrical highlight was a Sunday evening at the Royalty, where Sylvia Young Theatre School students danced energetically and sang lustily. More than two hundred were due to take part but a bug struck down forty of them. When did you last see a show with forty people off and no one noticed?

EN ROUTE FOR Edinburgh I ran into an old friend, the actress Chrissie Kendal. Some years ago I contributed to a correspondence in *The Times* about malaprops, having discovered Chrissie to be a queen among malapropers. Since then Philip Norman has collected some of the best in his book, *Your*

Walrus Hurt The One You Love. She calls the Royal Shakespeare Company the RAC; a friend went off to Israel to work on 'a kebab' and way back in 1979 she was concerned about the fate of 'the ostriches'. 'What ostriches, Chrissie?' 'The ostriches in prison in Iran.'

Deeply concerned for a friend and the Aids business she asked innocently, 'is he HP positive?' Realizing, as few malaprops do, that she had made an embarrassing error, she corrected herself. 'Sorry,' she said, 'I mean is he HMV positive?'

I had not been to the Edinburgh festival properly since 1963, when David Frost and I were asked to Kenneth Tynan's first writers' conference. All I can remember is 'happenings' in the Usher Hall and Lillian Hellman losing the 90,000-word ms of her account of the freedom march in Washington. We traced that to the airport; but she soon found another worry. Dame Judith Anderson had no tickets for Alec Guinness in Ionesco's *Exit the King* and thought it was Lillian's job to get them for her.

Much moaning by Ms Hellman. 'Actresses! Why do they expect writers to do everything for them?'

Some see it the other way.

I AM CONCERNED for Mrs Thatcher's future and, as I doubt if she has had much time to dwell on it of late, I have given it some thought. When she goes, what honours are available?

Let us start with the garter. This is very much the personal gift of the Queen, so Mrs T will have to tread carefully – if she wants to land one. Last year HM modified the order to include lady commoners. If Lavinia, Duchess of Norfolk, had not preceded her, Mrs T would have been the first non-royal since Edward III inaugurated the gong in 1348. According to Bluemantle Pursuivant she would be styled Lady Margaret Thatcher LG – to differentiate her from the daughters of dukes, marquesses and earls.

Raising the stakes, prime ministers have no automatic right to an earldom or dukedom. That, too, is in the gift of the

Crown, but several have taken earldoms. Countess of Grantham, with Mark to succeed, is pretty small beer. Duchess is nearer the target.

There are several precedents for the offer in the last hundred years. The Marquis of Salisbury (three times PM) declined a dukedom in 1892 with the unconvincing excuse that he couldn't afford it. King George V offered one to Lloyd George on Victoria Station when he returned from the peace conference in 1919. L-G also declined. So did Churchill in 1945.

Mrs T should take it. But in what name? Duchess of Finchley

and Duchess of Dulwich have too suburban a ring. Duchess of Downing Street would give the impression that she had never gone away, which might not be popular in some quarters. Duchess of Grantham is better, but let us not forget the Harry Cust connection aired earlier. Already Mrs Thatcher has the famous Belton silver at No 10 on loan from the National Trust. This indeed suggests a romantic connection. Why not Duchess of Belton? Mark could then be Marquis of the South Atlantic.

Denis, I fear, will get nothing except, perhaps, OM for services to golf. The nearest precedent for him is Spain, where a son-in-law can inherit his wife's family title. There, as in the old Hollywood, 'the son-in-law also rises'.

NO SOONER DO I solve the problem of Mrs Thatcher's title than I am faced with an even bigger conundrum, what was in the Duchess of York's 53 items of excess baggage when she landed at Heathrow after her visits to Texas and New York? Her jaunt was called a research trip by Buckingham Palace so we can soon expect a sequel to her *Budgie The Little Helicopter* books. I am betting the new title will be *Budgie's Friend Jumbo Gets Metal Fatigue*.

Obviously the thoughtful girl had done her Christmas shopping early at Nieman Marcus. The Texan store specializes in fabulous fancy goods for the very wealthy and is particularly big on 'his and her' gifts, so I suppose Fergie chose his and her choppers for herself and the Duke. Other lines include his and her submarines – for mother – and father-in-law? Silver salt and pepper shakers in the shape of howling coyotes 'for all at Kensington Palace'? A 'Concert Grand Marnier', a bar in the shape of a piano, at $6,600 – for Grandma Windsor? Then there are the world's smallest hot-air balloons, carried like a backpack for country walks with a difference. At $18,000 the pair, they would be perfect for Wills and Harry. Prince Edward is getting a customized Harley Davidson at $25,000, which he will find really useful, and the rest of the family can have the pick of his and her Chinese junks, ermine bathrobes or 2,000-year-old Egyptian mummy cases. Unwrapping the gifts at Sandringham this year should be fun.

THE DEATH of the redoubtable, charming Dame Peggy Shepherd struck a nostalgic note for me. When we piloted 'TW3' in 1962 she was chairman of the Conservative Women's National Advisory Committee. She led a group of Tory ladies whom Bernard Levin confronted on the programme. Five times one of them thundered at him: 'Mr Macmillan has always satisfied me!' Another woman was strident on law and order: 'Mr Levin, how would you like it if your daughter was up a dark lane late at night and nothing done about it?' Neither was Dame Peggy.

After the recording, Grace Wyndham Goldie gave the show her thumbs down. However the Tory ladies made such a fuss at Central Office about the depth of the depravity to which the pilot had sunk that a protest was lodged at the highest level of the BBC. More senior viewers monitored the experiment. Fortunately they found it vastly amusing and, thanks to Tory Central Office, we were booked for an initial 26 weeks.

FOR SCOTT'S RESTAURANT I secured this exclusive from a fishy film star, Wanda.

'It's not often a fish gets to play the title role in a movie. I recently co-starred with John Cleese in *A Fish Called Wanda*. I can't think of another piscatorial performer who has done it since my old friend Jaws; and as a piece of acting I think most people would agree with me that *Jaws* was way over the top of the tank. To call Jaws (as some critics have) the Donald Wolfit of the Deep is an insult to the great Shakespearean and a fine subtle film artist. The fact that they went on to make *Jaws II* is not so much of a tribute to the skill of the star as an indictment of the taste of mammal film makers.

Of course, coming as I do from a background of alternative fish comedy, I had to adjust to the stage and film techniques of stars like Maria Aitken and Kevin Kline and it took some time to get used to a director, Charles Crichton, who at eighty-plus was roughly the age of your average coelacanth. I found more sympathy with Cleese and Michael Palin, who have, after all, had some experience in the anarchic art of swim-up comedy. I've played some pretty odd aquaria in my time, I can tell you, but as long as there's a pair of punters prepared to put their fins together Wanda will never let them down.

Going legit has opened up new vistas of employment for me and I'm pleased to say there have been a lot of offers – some of them from overseas. A few were not in the best of taste and my agent advised me to say a very firm 'no' to a cameo role as the fish course in *Babette's Feast II*. He's anxious for me to develop my comedy talent and felt that stripping to the bone was not something that a fish of my quality should think of doing.

I was very touched to be asked to sing 'There's a Plaice for Us' in the upcoming revival of *West Side Story Under Water*. Underwater productions are all the new rage in the States and are rapidly replacing ice shows. Some of my best friends are skates, but one has to move with the times. Actually, I'm not going to do *West Side* in spite of the fact that Stephen Sondheim has re-written 'There's a Plaice ...' including the emotive line, 'Fondle my fins and I'll find you there', because I really see myself as a sole singer.

However, there are other exciting plans. We are going to option a new novel, *Satanic Perches*, by the popular author Salmon Rushdie, which has shot to the top of the best seller lists and my new agents PBAM (Piranha and Barracuda Artists Management) are developing a new concept in soaps with an everyday story of amphibious folk; and also the first 'Fish n' Chatshow' which will take place in an original pub setting which we are calling the 'Whelk and Winkle'. John Cleese has asked if he can be on the first programme but I feel that would be too incestuous. I sometimes think I'm being used and that Cleese is just after publicity. I have to preserve my image and I'm not sure that the right way to do that is to have guests endlessly playing the fool.

I was delighted to see old Crichton receiving an award on the BAFTA programme even though he omitted to mention me, but, as they say, old men forget. I'm wondering what his next project will be and if there's a role in it for me. I was a little disturbed to read a profile of him in the *Independent* the other week. It sounds as though he's been on another talent hunt. If I may quote, it says, 'The rest of the time he likes to go fishing. He used to haunt the reservoirs near London in a small rowing boat, but had to give this up when his back became so painful he couldn't even walk. Now he fishes from the banks of Scottish and Welsh rivers and his new-found prosperity has enabled him to plan to take the whole of this summer doing so.'

Now, obviously no grown man is going to spend a whole summer on a river bank unless he has a serious purpose in mind. It sounds to me like the biggest talent search since they were looking for a Scarlett O'Hara for *Gone With the Wind*. Perhaps they're thinking of doing *Gone With the Water*, and if they are I don't want to hear that tired old excuse 'We're looking for a young Wanda.' There's plenty of life in the old Wanda.

Perhaps I should make this an open letter to reputable film producers. Just ask me along to Scott's for a little light luncheon, nothing elaborate, a simple fly and watercress salad, a platter of *plankton thermidor* and I'll be happy to discuss your project. It isn't every British star who's nominated for an Oscar in their first movie.'

A Little Light Relief

Having opened in World's End, let us round off with
Australia and a rich vein of Australian humour
(another oxymoron?)

I discovered that light bulb jokes are popular there – as in,
'How many Country and Western stars does it take to change
a light bulb?'

'Ten. One to change it, and nine to sing about what a good
ol' bulb it was.'

This set the lines between home and Deal humming on my
return, as my man there and I tried to decide how many
Scottish judges it takes to change a light bulb. We did not
think that ten (one to change it and nine to do the Gay
Gordons) was good enough.

We moved on. As the Neil, Worsthorne, Bordes trial kept
people happy, many of us became concerned about how many
editors it takes to change a bulb. There were some conflicting
views. Some held the traditional opinion that it takes ten. One
who does it, one who wishes he could do it, one who remembers
George Melly doing it, and seven who can't wait to write
about it. A more economical approach suggested that it can
be done by four: one to do it, one who would like to do it, one
who complains of other people doing it, and one who paid
£500 to do it.

Investigating further, I tried to get MI5 to confirm how
many of their dirty tricks officers it takes to change a light
bulb. At first they stonewalled, 'None, we prefer to leave
you in the dark.' However, a hard-pressed spokesman finally

admitted that in the case of the screw-in bulbs it takes two. One to hold it, while a Russian colleague turns him.

Then a mole rang to tell me that it only takes one, but it takes fifteen years for the light to come on.

Finally, as Mike Tyson hit the canvas, I started to research the number of boxing referees it takes to change one but got no joy from the British Boxing Board of Control. However, Neil Shand, my boxing correspondent, told me it is any number between ten and thirteen depending on who's counting. Alternatively, the total is ten but you can add a couple of seconds from Buster Douglas's corner. As my social correspondent, he also revealed how many Donald Trumps it takes. The answer is one, but the light bulb has to be fifteen years younger.

PS. Q: How many feminists does it take to change a light bulb?
A: *That's* not funny!

p 76   Ms Storme's agent has subsequently written to say that she never auditioned for *Aspects of Love*.

p 129   The following letter from Gore Vidal appeared in *The Times* on 2 September 1989:

Sir, Ned Sherrin writes (Review, August 26) that I "have developed a consuming interest in the Prime Minister's forebears". For the record, I have no interest in anyone's forebears, including my own, save for a milk joke about Nether Wallop.

Before a radio broadcast, Sherrin and I were chatting about the mysteries of English life, and I said that the preoccupation with who was who's real ancestor was even more boring than to be told who was going to bed with whom among one's non-acquaintances. The Thatcher story was used as a recent example of what is making the rounds, and not for publication.

Also, for the record my father was never "Douglas Fairbanks Senior's gym coach": in 1923, Mr Vidal was starting an airline called TWA. As I wrote recently in the press, the beauty of TV-radio is one's direct contact with the public "without the smothering intervention of a print-journalist bent on re-creating one to conform to his publisher's prejudices".

Yours faithfully,
GORE VIDAL,
Ravello, Salerno,
Italy.
August 30.

DEREK NIMMO

TABLE TALK

Presented with the very private parts of a curried goat in Nigeria, suffering childhood picnics on the sleet-swept Pennine moors, escaping, half-starved from a health farm to gorge on a butter-oozing, calorie uncontrolled feast, recalling the wise and witty sayings of the great chefs, hosts, gourmets and gannets of the past: Derek Nimmo's Table Talk is a delicious, bubbling bouillabaisse of strange ingredients and unusual anecdotes.

After-dinner stories and under-the-table revelations, recipes for disaster and menus for merriment, from Victorian blowouts to the mean, lean cuisine of today: with Derek Nimmo at your elbow, you're never more than a soup-spill away from catastrophe and farce . . .

POST A LITTLE HAPPINESS

Post·A·Book

A Royal Mail service in association with the Book Marketing Council & The Booksellers Association.

Post-A-Book is a Post Office trademark.

BEPPE SEVERGNINI

INGLESI

Translated by Paola Pugsley

Do the British really hate washing so much?

There has been a torrent of comment and discussion in recent months about the British attitude to Europe. But what do the Europeans think of the British?

From East Anglia to the Hebrides, from Brighton to Belfast, taking in Royal Ascot, Blackpool, Wembley dog-track and a host of other sacred venues, Beppe Severgnini has travelled the land to produce a fascinating portrait of the British people and their habits as others see them.

Hard-hitting, hilarious, provocative, informative, *Inglesi* is essential reading for the British — and their neighbours!

HODDER AND STOUGHTON PAPERBACKS

DAVID RENWICK

BUT I DIGRESS

**The collected monologues of
ramblin' Ronnie Corbett**

"Tonight I've been asked to be brief. And they don't
come much briefer . . . To be honest, I haven't been so
nervous since I found myself standing in the Gents next
to Shakin' Stevens . . . I actually heard this story while I
was sitting in a box full of Action Men, entertaining the
troops . . . it was next to an article entitled 'What to do if
you hunger after sex: keep a packet of biscuits on the
bedside table' . . ."

Once again it's Hello From Him as RONNIE CORBETT
meanders back through 50 of his hilariously rambling
monologues from the big armchair on The Two Ronnies,
proving that the longest distance between two points is
a series of very funny lines.

But I Digress is the cream of his anecdotes and stories,
plus one or two old yoghurts. Re-live them and laugh all
over again.

HODDER AND STOUGHTON PAPERBACKS

ROBERT MORLEY

AROUND THE WORLD IN 81 YEARS

'Unmistakably honest and hugely funny'
Sunday Telegraph

It all started at Folkestone.

'On rough days Nurse would take us down to the harbour ... where we found sea-sick passengers in a woebegone huddle boarding waiting trains. "That's what comes of going abroad, Master Robert," she would tell me.'

But to Act is perforce to Travel.

The young Robert Morley, learning his craft in provincial touring companies, discovers that in England all journeys involve a Sunday afternoon change at Crewe.

Later come location shoots in exotic foreign parts with exotic foreign weather. Nature, he realises, abhors the film maker and teases the tourist. Ayers Rock resolutely refuses to turn pink at dawn. The Niagara Falls are closed for repairs ...

Around the World in 81 Years is a delightful voyage through times and places, packed with anecdotes and asides, by a man who loved life but basically found it all part of the theatre of the absurd.

'A delight to leaf through ... the perfect travelling companion'
Film Review

HODDER AND STOUGHTON PAPERBACKS

MORE TITLES AVAILABLE FROM
HODDER AND STOUGHTON PAPERBACKS